Glimpse

Dan Hix

Parson's Porch Books

Glimpse
ISBN: Softcover 978-1-960326-97-3
Copyright © 2024 by Dan Hix

Parson's Porch Books is an imprint of Parson's Porch *&* Company (PP*&*C) in Cleveland, Tennessee. PP*&*C is a self-funded charity which earns money by publishing books of noted authors, representing all genres. Its face and voice is **David Russell Tullock** who you can contact at: dtullock@parsonsporch.com.

Parson's Porch *&* Company *turns books into bread & milk* by sharing its profits with the poor.

www.parsonsporch.com

Glimpse

Contents

Introduction

"For me writing has always felt like praying."

Marilynne Robinson in GILEAD

No one is more surprised than I am to see my name on the front of a book. While I have done my share of writing, like most ministers, the kind of writing you see in this book didn't start stirring for me till well into my mid-fifties when I landed at Saint Mary's Hospital in Knoxville, TN as chaplain. In fact, I blame this urge, this emerging, rather recent call to write on the Sisters of Mercy whose welcome included the expectation to take my turn in the tradition of morning prayer delivered over the PA in that sacred, ancient place. I quickly grew tired of my old style of more spontaneous public prayer, began to be more intentional, listening more deeply, and then writing my prayers - that was the start of something I did not see coming. Surprisingly, many of the prayers came to me as kind of a poem and patients and staff began to ask for copies. I was moved to realize something I had been inspired to write was touching someone else. And it went on from there. Thank you Sisters – just one of the many ways that remarkable and devoted group enriched my life.

She's usually my first reader. Pam, my partner in life, has probably read most everything I have written – a true labor of love. She's a good editor, sometimes too good, often exasperated by my lack of skill in grammar and punctuation. Believe me, I've heard it more than once, "Were you absent the day they taught commas?" But Pam's also my most enthusiastic encourager, and she's the best way I know to measure if something I have written amounts to anything worthwhile. If I put it in front of her, and after a few minutes of silence I notice tears running down her cheek, then I know the mysterious blessing, the reassurance I have produced something I need to hold on to, something worth sharing. Without Pam's open heart and constant, long-suffering pushing, this book simply would not exist.

Wendell Berry, in his wonderful poem, "How To Be a Poet," writes: "Any readers who like your poems, doubt their judgment." Now, that's funny, yet I hear the warning as well as the wisdom of Berry's line. But what if they cry, what if your reader cries, what if by some wonder words you wrote carry someone inexplicably beyond words, even to worship? Who wouldn't feel fortunate – who wouldn't feel privileged, to be part of a meaningful experience like that?

Dan

A Glimpse of the Kingdom

"There is neither Jew nor Greek, there is neither slave nor free, there is neither male nor female; for you are all one in Christ Jesus." Galatians 3:28

"The Kingdom of Heaven comes in small steps."
Mac Wallace, CPE Supervisor, NCBH, 1982

One of the joys of going into work a little late is the opportunity to carve out an hour in a local coffee shop to read, think, and enjoy something for breakfast besides yogurt. Working in Knoxville and for the last few years having no kids in Maryville Schools, I sometimes feel like I only sleep in Maryville and am alienated from the life of this great community. So, it is a treat to look around and realize I have been neighbor to some of the folks in that place for 30 years. In fact, I often see a man there who is about my age. He has three sons who played AYSO soccer with Andrew 25 years ago. He does not have a clue who I am when I smile and speak to him, but it feels good to remember.

I quickly learned to avoid a certain corner of the shop because a group of men congregates there every morning, pontificates on, and solves all the problems of the world, and my goodness, they are loud. You can only imagine, with all of the chaos in our country, they have a lot to chew on, debate, and disagree about. But somehow, even with their loud arguments, they obviously remain friends. A while back they surprised me. As I overheard their conversation, and believe me it is not hard to overhear, I realized they were discussing their various churches; not complaining, but clearly involved, concerned, knowledgeable, and supportive of their pastors. And in one case that pastor happened to be a woman. Who would have thought? I was suddenly hopeful and felt badly for whatever presumptions I made. For everyone who worries about the lack of male involvement in church, I wish you could hear what I heard. It almost made me want to be a pastor again...almost. But my goodness, they are loud.

Then they surprised me again. I had another chance to go in late, stopped by the coffee shop and, of course, they were in their spot.

But this time there was a new face in the group, just as loud and opinionated as everyone else, but this face was African American. I regret calling him out in that way. Perhaps the day will finally come when we do not make a point of distinguishing; it is my constant prayer. But there he was totally involved, totally included. I am grateful I can carry that picture in my memory because sometimes I grow weary and lose heart; recently despairing losing ground in the struggle for respect and tolerance. That loud group of guys was a well of encouragement to me. You are right, Mac, small steps. I think I heard the Kingdom heading in my direction in a coffee shop in Maryville and it sounded like a rowdy bunch of open-hearted, old men.

A Kind of Awakening

"It makes me wonder what they think of me." Every year when we arrive at Black History month this moment, this sacred encounter comes back to me. While I know and am grateful, while I celebrate there is more to the Black experience in this country than racism, I find it personally necessary to grieve the price paid and to remind myself of the ongoing cost of intolerance, so much of it an invisible wound, really unimaginable to someone whose skin is the color of mine. So, I'm in some ways haunted - I remember and inwardly cringe - I'm back in the hospital cafeteria again, early in the morning, seated across the table, listening to those grief-filled, yet deeply defiant words, filled with years, really a lifetime of enduring, brokenhearted weariness: "It makes me wonder what they think of me."

She is one of the most gracious, one of the strongest, most devout people in my life. I have known her forever, for over 30 years, blessed to call her my friend, often marveling at her capacity to face challenges with determination and faith, so many of us beneficiaries of her warmth and support, her hard-won wisdom. But this was a searing glimpse, a kind of sacred access into a burden she carries every moment of every day; an insidiously vile burden I cannot pretend to understand. Though the temptation is to look away, to foster a myth, to rewrite history, she would not allow it; she quietly, courageously raised my unconscious white presumption up before me and it broke my heart.

Because of the arbitrariness of the artificial designation of race and the damage of generations of evil, willful ignorance, I am free of the uncertainty, and at times fear, she regularly feels when intolerance and disrespect are the intentional and unintentional currency of our discourse. I am not personally threatened when White Nationalism informs public policy and pollutes the rhetoric of some of the most powerful in the land; disrespect cynically manipulated, stirring then reaching deep into the cesspool of mistrust of difference, unconstrained by truth, willing to say anything, ready to do whatever to fuel political gain. I do not have to question when coworkers or even friends either openly or tacitly support or defend the racist agenda of our leaders in everyday banter or by simply saying nothing. I do not have to privately struggle and wonder, "If they believe, if they support that, what do they think of me and those I love?"

Moved, tears, it was a kind of awakening. That ordinary spot, suddenly, uncomfortably, made holy.

Affirming What's Lost

I whisper over to myself the way of loss, the names of the dead. One by one, we lose our loved ones, our friends, our powers of work and pleasure, our landmarks, the days of our allotted time. One by one the way we lose them, they return to us and are treasured up in our hearts. Grief affirms them, preserves them, sets the cost.

-Wendell Berry in JAYBER CROW

To live in this world
you must be able to do three things:
to love what is mortal:
to hold it
against your bones knowing
your own life depends on it;
and, when the time comes, to let it go
to let it go.

-Mary Oliver in "In Blackwater Woods"

I miss the drawing
Welcome laboring toward each new day
Miss holy anticipation rising, gathering
Wonder receiving waking dawn
Morning after morning stirring hope
Today's the day live faithful to calling
Today we'll bring some light
Today we'll do some good.

I miss the ramble, unhurried, unprescribed
Though urgent, "in midst of trouble," I miss the saunter
Listening, bearing witness, I miss the holy stroll.

I miss the banter, miss even the outrage
I miss the protests, desperate, even futile hopes
Quick, deep vulnerability, miss openhearted love.

I miss compassion palpable, miss compassion embodied
Meaning-filled, the exhausting depletion
The weary purpose, I miss the holy fatigue.

I miss the surprise, miss incomprehensible shock
Witness, life's resilience, witness, life's mystery
Witness, holy finality, death's silent, perplexing hush.

I miss examples, miss models innumerable
Holy, hinting, living grace's persistence
Mercy's brave triumph though cure eludes.

I miss colleagues, miss my friends
I miss the trust, the hugs
The respect, the pure privilege '
I miss the holy membership.

I miss, well, sometimes, bewildered
Miss it all, sometimes, suddenly miss it all
But never gratitude, never miss gratitude
Carried safely, carefully affirmed
Blessing claimed
Fixed forever in my heart.

Against Any Wind

"We inhabit a world of cynicism and snark, of hopelessness and dread. These are our demons. They close off our imaginations, they isolate us from hope and always tempt us to believe the worst. Eventually, we give in because we don't want more disappointment, more broken promises, more hurt. Nothing will change. Taunting is easier."

-Diana Butler Bass in "Sunday Musings, January 28"

"Help me please to carry
this candle against the wind."

-Wendell Berry

We're moving ahead, Lord
We're moving ahead, but wary, but exhausted
We're moving ahead, expectations faltering
Moving ahead, but with diminishing hope
Howling winds batter, flickering light struggles
Near extinguished, desperately unequal
Against winds of self-centeredness and greed
Against winds of threats and violence
Against winds of intolerance and disrespect
Dishonoring truth, ridiculing integrity.

We're moving ahead, Lord
We're moving ahead, and we wonder
Anxious, cannot help but wonder

Will darkness big, darkness unimaginably bad
Inevitable, will darkness overcome, finally snuff out
Darkness suffocate tiny, trembling light
We wonder, anxious, cannot help but wonder
Will darkness have the final word?

We're moving ahead, Lord
We're moving ahead, though consider
Intimidated by all the facts
How vast the darkness, how small our light
How tangled the wilderness, how bewildered our hearts
But, we're moving ahead, Lord
We're moving ahead, mustering trust
Where we are weak, you are strong
Where we are lost, where dead end rises
Walls push in, barriers close round
Even there you approach, enter, you never abandon
Calling and calling, you patiently bear
Accompany against the wind
Against any wind.

We're moving ahead, Lord.

Always Coming

A voice cries: "In the wilderness prepare the way of the Lord, make straight in the desert a highway for our God."

Isaiah 40:3

Lord you call, then keep calling
Patient, call persistent
Raising your voice wherever I am
Even here, in maddening wilderness
You speak into chaotic darkness
Waken longing, you call my name
Then call again, then call again.
But, impatient, I struggle, a clumsy listener
Distracted, desperate for satisfaction
Sometimes convinced wealth is answer
Grasping more, building portfolio
Yet, emptiness rises, voice cries out
Sometimes lured by safety's illusion
Suspecting everyone, defending everywhere
Yet, wariness builds, anxiety intrudes
Sometimes enticed, persuaded pleasure fulfills
Seeking excitement, craving entertainment
Yet, discontent abides, troubling, demanding
For beneath frantic noise

Still, small voice, your voice, urging, drawing
Have mercy, did not know it was you.

Lord you call, then keep calling
On the move
Steadfast, you move my direction
No matter how lost
How far off beaten path
Coming, coming, deep into wilderness
Driven, you keep coming my way
Dismissive barriers
Regardless, prepared or not
Coming, coming, deep into wilderness
Driven, you keep coming my way
Challenging rigid certainty
Narrow, spirit-withering agenda
Relentless, you pursue
Wooing, wooing, seek till you find
Determined to capture my heart
Mission to liberate my soul.

Lord you call, then keep calling
Patient, call persistent
I wait
Wait restless, wait hungry
Hungrier than I know
Wait ear pressed to the ground.

Amen.

And Brave

Love is patient and kind; love is not jealous or boastful; it is not arrogant or rude. Love does not insist on its own way; it is not irritable or resentful; it does not rejoice at wrong, but rejoices in the right. Love bears all things, hopes all things, endures all things. Love never ends.

1 Corinthians 13:4-8

"To love the world as much even as I could love it would be suffering also, for I would fail. And yet all the good I know is in this, that a man might so love this world that it would break his heart."

Wendell Berry in JAYBER CROW

Yes, agree with Paul
Cranky Saint, why, he's relieved, I'm sure
Yes, believe Paul's right
Righter than Hallmark
Righter than fairy tales
Righter, than "Bachelor" or "Bachelorette"
Yes, so much righter than "Bachelor" or Bachelorette"
Yes, believe Paul's right
Absolutely right on love
Yes, love's patient, love's kind
Not jealous, not boastful, not lot of things
Yes, love bears, believes, hopes
Yes, love defiant, love endures all things
Yes, love never ends, never let's you go
Yes, Paul's right, all that, every bit's true.

But this too, yes, this true as well
Love exposes
Love reveals
Love harrows
Love scares you to death

Love can make you brave
Calling toward uncertain edge
Urging through silent, darkest night
Dare follow, and fair warning
Dare follow, and love makes you brave
Reckless, strangely openhearted
Vulnerable, so vulnerable, startlingly brave
Braver than ever been
Braver than imagined could be
Yes, love makes you brave.

Can't deny it, for I've seen it
Maybe you have too
Faithful, exhausted at bedside
Helpless, but holding
Holding, holding long as it takes
Holding to the end
Can't deny it, for I've seen it
Vigilant, searching, then searching again
Unreasonable, hoping, then hoping again
Wondering, praying, then praying again
Let this be the morning
Let this be the day
Lost wandering
Beloved soul finally, finally comes home.

Yes, blessed to see it
Maybe you too
Even against my will, opened
Slowly, slowly changed by it
Love breaks your heart
Love makes you brave
Braver than ever been
Braver than imagined could be
Terribly, wonderfully brave.

All the good I know.

Angel Unaware

Do not neglect to show hospitality to strangers, for thereby some have entertained angels unawares. Hebrews 13:2

To attach oneself to place is to surrender to it, and suffer with it
-Kathleen Norris in CLOISTER WALK

"Hey Dan, do you know anything about the person sleeping on the sidewalk?" I was making rounds through the main lobby Thursday morning when one of our staff expressed concern. Well, it is difficult to ignore an observation like that, so I went to see what might be going on, silently praying I found nothing. But, sure enough, I caught sight of whoever it was from the top of the hill on Saint Mary's Street, crouching under a blue blanket next to a parking meter, just a few feet from Fulton High's football field. So, I started down the hill with no plan, thinking of all that could go wrong once I reached him or her. At first, I hoped it was just a pile of clothes, but then glimpsed part of a face, and after several loud greetings, much to my relief, she woke up, squinting at me; a pretty young woman with a huge bruised eye and a poorly healed scar running from her temple to her neck; one of God's children, someone's troubled daughter. She told me her name was Jennifer. Everything I suggested, she resisted or outright rejected. No, she was not sick. No, she did not want a bus ticket to the mission. No, she did not have family for me to call. And just as my old knees had reached their limit from kneeling down beside her, I realized Ashley had followed me down the hill. If there is a kinder person in our hospital, I do not know who it is. There she was with the same warmth and smile with which she greets patients and those who love them, helpful in every way. So, one more time I went through my list of options with Jennifer, and one more time she declined, until I asked if I could get her breakfast and she nodded her head affirmatively. "I'll stay with her," Ashley volunteered. "Oh, you don't need to do that, Ashley," I

23

countered, "It will take me a bit to get to the cafeteria and back down here. You don't need to stay." "I'll stay," she said firmly. To be honest, I was instantly aware Ashley had chosen the hardest work and guiltily relieved to have an excuse to leave the scene for a few minutes.

So, I chugged back up the hill, ran to the Cafe, and began the walk back down Saint Mary's Street. I wish I had a picture of the scene coming into focus at the bottom of the hill. In fact, in this day of ubiquitous cell phones, I almost took a photo, but it just did not seem right. Because what I had the privilege of witnessing was what for all the world looked like the presence of an angel – not Jennifer, I really do not know enough about her to call her an angel, that's up to God, but Ashley – God's quiet, open-hearted presence in the dust and grime of the street. In the time I was gone, Ashley made herself "comfortable" on the curb right beside Jennifer, right on her level, and what's more, found a way to win this suspicious, hurting, hungry woman's trust. I could see them chatting, and as I grew closer, heard them, the warm sound of caring, human conversation. I am thinking Jennifer has experienced far too few of those in her short, difficult life.

The need at our doorstep at Physician's Regional Medical Center, our beloved Saint Mary's, is overwhelming, unremitting. As we prepare to abandon Oak Hill, I keep being reminded there was a reason those courageous, faithful Sisters of Mercy began their ministry there decades ago, investing their gifts and lives in work which was never going to make sense in the cutthroat world of healthcare business. On Thursday morning that intimidating, grinding need, source of predatory profit for the unscrupulous, ignored by the powerful, politicized by legislators; that need the Sisters would recognize; that need they selflessly labor to ameliorate, showed up again in broken flesh and blood, and although still just as jarring, complicated, and intractable as ever, thanks to the grace and mercy of Ashley, and some scrambled eggs and biscuits and gravy, along with a pair of tennis shoes Ashley managed to rustle, one young woman's world changed – at least for a little while, at least for that morning. And then...God only knows. I can imagine the Sisters of Mercy knowingly smiling in approval, joyfully bearing burdens to the end, their generous, committed witness accompanying, leading ahead.

Angels in Baldwin

Any father (particularly an old father) must finally give his child up to the wilderness and trust to the providence of God. Great faith is required to give the child up, trusting God to honor the parents' love for him by assuring that there will be angels in that wilderness.

-Marilynne Robinson in GILEAD

We are all as little children, some know it and some don't.

-Wendell Berry in "Pray Without Ceasing"

For I am sure that neither death, nor life, nor angels, nor principalities, nor things present, nor things to come, nor powers, not height, nor depth, nor anything else in all creation, will be able to separate us from the love of God in Christ Jesus our Lord.

Romans 8:28

"You do realize you have an angel, don't you?" I didn't know Diane very well and was caught off guard. She was on a short assignment, a contract, at the hospital. From out of town, away from her family, and lonely in the evening, she asked if she could meet my wife, Pam, and me for dinner. So, while waiting for our order to arrive, Diane looked across the booth and repeated, much to my discomfort, "Yes, you have an angel. She's right behind you, beautiful, with long, blonde hair." Pam looked at me, raising her eyebrows with what I chose to interpret as amused suspicion. "An angel?" I thought. "Obviously Diane does not know my cynicism when it comes to all the popular fascination with angels."

But it wasn't long till Baldwin, Wisconsin happened. That isolated spot near the Minnesota state line is not the best place to be stranded by a flat tire, in the dark, by the Interstate, surrounded by snow, with January temperatures plunging below zero. I was helping Andrew move to Minneapolis for an internship – well, I am not sure how much I was helping, but I was at least along for the ride. The old Camry was crammed to the gills and the only thing resembling a spare under all that stuff was one of those donut jobs. And did I mention it was pitch black and freezing? Earlier, I had just about convinced myself I really did not need to be on this trip; that in fact, tagging along was just the last ditch expression of over-invested parenthood. And in some ways I suppose it really was something like that. But no one should have to face a moment like this one alone. Maybe Andrew did not need his dad along, but he needed someone – we both did. And as it turned out, we were not by ourselves, there were "angels in that wilderness," to quote Marilynne Robinson.

First angel we met was a tow driver sent by AAA. How he ever found us miles from the nearest exit I will never know. He showed up, hazard lights flashing, dressed for the weather in a yellow snow suit, and after crawling through the ice and slush, attaching a cable here and one there, had our disabled car on his truck in no time. He was funny, competent, and confident we would find a solution, driving us into the small town of Baldwin, where we met the second angel at a dark, warehouse looking building with the name "Shalom Valley Tire Services" plastered on the outside. It looked like a good setting for a horror movie and I could not help but wonder, "If something happens to us out here, who will ever know?" The mechanic was tall, bearded, covered with piercings and tattoos and spoke at a clip and with an accent my Southern ears had a hard time identifying as English. But first impressions aside, he also turned out to be an angel. He had been long gone from work on a Friday night, clean and warm, but came back to that freezing place to take care of us. In fact, I was astounded when he asked, "Here's how much the new tire costs (because we did manage to destroy the old one), but what do you think would be a fair service charge?" I do not guess he could have chosen a more appropriate name for his business, "Shalom"... God's peace. God's messengers come near in unexpected ways and he was one of them.

Perhaps I do have an angel after all, maybe even multiple angels — everybody needs help sometime and some of us need more divine assistance than others. But the angels in Wisconsin, at least the angels I encountered, were far from Hallmark Christmas card worthy, hardly beautiful, at least in any way that should worry Pam. But here's the good news, they were just what we needed, they were angels familiar with wilderness. Good thing, for whether we accept it or not, we all wander into wilderness from time to time, probably not in frigid Baldwin, Wisconsin, but no one is immune from wilderness; it has a way of finding us. And once there, stumbling around in wilderness, even as unpleasant and nerve-rattling as it is, we have the opportunity to learn again, we are all children, all lost and searching, all overwhelmed and in need of help, but more beloved, more accompanied than we imagine — we are not alone.

Assaulted by Resurrection

They walk among us
Neighbor, friend, even enemy
Carrying mostly silenced stories
Walled away, driven down
Stowed, shredded, nailed closed
Hiding injury, brokenness, shame
Bruised and battered
Used and discarded
Stifling suffocated, inaudible screams
They walk among us
Carefully, quietly, bearing secrets
Haunted, never certain where
High alert, for never certain when
Next unexpected moment
Next step, tripping, triggering
Next callous joke
Next story ridiculed
Next pulpit trumpeting submission
Next headline ripping scab
Exposing wounds never healed.

O, Christ, like lamb to slaughter
Smitten, despised and rejected
You are not alone in resurrection
Grief rises again
Violent disrespect rises again
Insidious abuse rises again
Then rises again and again.

I've known her forever
Funny, compassionate, intense
My friend, my colleague in healing
I've known her forever
But not like this

Exhausted, expressionless
Extending shaking hand
Wrestling, beaten down by panic
Revisited by violation
Pray, Dan, she mumbled, pray
No…can't talk…makes it worse
Just pray.

Where is he?
Does he ever have sleepless night?
A moment, just a moment of regret?
Does he even remember?
For, I learned something yesterday
Something did not want to know
Something should have always known
My friend, my wonderful friend
My friend never forgets
She can't.

So, in helpless rage I will pray
How long, O Lord?

Bell Ringer

Matthew 20:26

"You might have to swing it two or three times before the clapper would strike. And then it struck: 'Dong!' And then around the sound of the clapper striking, the sound of the bell bloomed out in all directions over the countryside, into all the woods and hollows. It was never easy for me to stop ringing the bell, I so delighted in that interval of pure sound between the clapper strokes. The bell, I thought, voiced the best sermon of the day; it included everything, and in a way blessed it."

-Wendell Berry in JAYBER CROW

"I just like the way it sounds, and I think it is important. Maybe some of the folks who cannot come to church will hear and be encouraged."

-Kenneth Paxton, Bell Ringer, New Providence Presbyterian Church

I agree with Wendell Berry
For most part think old Jayber true
Almost, just about, pretty close
True, but one exception
One very important exception
For there is a better sermon
More beautiful, more life-changing
Better than booming, blessing bell
Sermon as steady witness
Proclaim, but quiet, yet revolutionary

Message, counter-cultural incarnation
Sermon as humble, committed life.

I know someone like that
Faithful, near anonymous
Never about him
About praise
About being noticed
About boosting reputation
No, always about service
Trustworthy light, a little hope
Good news in broken, discouraged world
I know someone like that
Great where matters most
Great in Kingdom of Heaven.

Some sermons stay with us always
Some ring on and on
Nudge insistently, call gently ahead
Showing, not just telling
Draw toward better way
I know sermon like that
We are accompanied, we are blessed
Lives made rich by good example
Surrounded, influenced by graciousness
We heard you, Mr. Paxton
We heard you and are encouraged.

Beloved Rascal of Mercy

When the Lord saw that he turned aside to see, God called to him out of the bush, "Moses, Moses!" And he said, "Here am I." Then he said, "Do not come near; put off your shoes from your feet, for the place on which you are standing is holy ground."

Exodus 3:4-5

"Justice is the grammar of things. Mercy is the poetry of things."

-Frederick Buechner

"I call her 'Rascal,'" BJ said with a smile. "Rascal, just seems to fit her, don't you think?" And I had to agree. But "Rascal"? Though fitting, wait just a minute, Albertine was a Sister, for goodness sake, a Sister of Mercy, with a long career as a devoted teacher and leader, a wealth of experience in ministry, serious ministry. Still, when it comes to mercy, you never quite get what you expect, certainly not what you deserve, and no one I know enjoyed delivering that surprise more than Sister Albertine, smart, direct, she did not hesitate to "tell you the truth" and love you at the same time. Sister Albertine, our beloved rascal of mercy, ornery, forceful channel of God's delight.

And yesterday was no different, Sister's funeral mass was filled with the unexpected, at least for me - I was wonderfully off balance all the way through. I expected to grieve – one does not lose a friend, a colleague so worthy of respect, so filled with selfless passion for God's Kingdom and not grieve. We miss her, we will always miss her. And I expected to be impressed – the review, our thanksgiving for her long, faithful life astounded, the setting, the ritual stunning,

33

all so moving, so inspiring as we were led along by incredibly gifted folks. I think I was prepared, pretty much expected all of that. But I should have known better than to have become too comfortable when it comes to anything Sister Albertine has a hand in. Because as we approached the conclusion, the service went to another level, it became personal, blessedly, uncomfortably personal for me. For while I expected to grieve my friend, and while I expected to be impressed, I did not expect to be overwhelmed, near struck down with a kind of inexpressible joy and gratitude. Suddenly, I do not think it is too strong to say, I was ambushed, I was a Baptist renegade captured by the Spirit in a Catholic Cathedral. There have been few times in my life when I have felt more out of control, more in the presence of overpowering mystery. For I did not expect Father Humbrecht to read some words I had written as a tribute to Sister Albertine over her casket before the recessional. It was humbling, it was emotional, it was an affirming gift. And I did not expect Father Thomas O'Connell to wave me out of the pew and into the impressively long line of Catholic clergy as they led Sister's casket toward the back of the great church. "Come join us. Walk with us. You are included. You belong." I was floored by gracious welcome. And I did not expect to be invited to join other clergy and friends sprinkling Sister's casket, "A sign of her baptism," a reminder while Albertine is certainly by vocation and through her whole giving life a Sister of Mercy, she is my sister as well, united in baptism, made one in Christ, members one of another. I know it is an overused description, but I have never been more convinced, like Moses, I was standing on Holy Ground.

Like all truly sacred, truly unexpected moments, there is no making complete sense out of what happened to me yesterday. I know beyond doubt I will be thinking about it and reflecting on it, I will be encouraged by it for the rest of my life. But I do know this for certain, no one was more amused and pleased by my perplexed, indescribable wonder than Sister Albertine, that joyful rascal, celebrant of the chaos of grace, poetic practitioner of wide, wide mercy. I'm still not quite sure how to adequately express my thanks...but Mercy's that way...held in Mercy's light, mere words fail.

Benedictions

The Lord bless you and keep you:

The Lord make his face to shine upon you, and be gracious to you:

The Lord lift up his countenance upon you, and give you peace.

Numbers 6:24-26

Just when you thought the afternoon could not be more gray, the weather more miserable as we gathered at the graveside, it began to rain, seriously peppering down, echoing off the funeral home canvas cover, moving family and friends closer together, huddling, seeking shelter. While focusing, while attempting to listen more carefully above the noise, I was startled to realize a perspective I don't normally have – in looking down, just at my feet, I could see all the way to the very bottom, to the clay floor of the dark, freshly dug grave. Against my will, the end, ever approaching mortality undeniably captured my uneasy attention. But then, well then, hope unexpected, hope resilient bore witness, thankfully a reminder there is more to the story, as a beautiful, clear voice from one standing under an umbrella out in the rain sang out Charles Wesley's faith filled, trusting plea.

Finish then, Thy new creation;
pure and spotless let us be;
let us see Thy great salvation
perfectly restored in Thee.
Changed from glory into glory,
till in heav'n we take our place,
till we cast our crowns before Thee,
lost in wonder, love, and praise.*

It was benediction; out of our damp grief and gloom, it seemed the Lord's face shown upon us. But surprising wonder wasn't through with me yet, for just minutes later I was standing a few miles away in my friend's room at the nursing facility. I knew he would be asleep. He's approaching the end of his long life and graciously, he appears comfortable, peacefully sleeping. I agree with Wendell Berry's observation that "it's not a tragedy when an old man dies at the end of his life," but still, the bonds of affection and respect call for acknowledgment – and believe me, there is much to celebrate in the 107 years my friend has been among the living. So yesterday, I went quickly by knowing he would not be able to respond to me, but feeling a need to just be in his presence and express my thanks.

Our visits have been memorable, often leaving me grateful and somewhat in awe. Between his almost total deafness and my challenges in handwriting, our "conversations" can be an effort, but worth it. I carefully print out what I want to try to say, and after reading my painful script, he always answers with a wonderful, strong, Mississippi Delta accent. He has had a remarkable life and I enjoy his stories immensely. A couple of weeks ago I asked him how Ole' Miss was doing in football. He loves to talk football. "Well," he responded, and I could hear the pride in his voice. "Let me show you." Whereupon he picked up the paper and read through the most recent rankings. "Well, Georgia is number one. That's good, they have a good team. I always pull for teams from the SEC unless they are playing Ole' Miss." Then carefully making his way down the list, he came to his beloved school. "And Ole' Miss is number 10.

Number 10! That's good! That's pretty good!" "It sure is," I answered.

While in his near silent, his shadowed room yesterday, as my friend slowly labored toward death, and the cold rain poured outside the window, the nurse came quietly in to give the next dose of his medication. He did not stir, just slept peacefully on. "He doesn't rouse," she said. "Even when we turn him, he sleeps." But then, before she left, she leaned down close to his ear and whispered, "You sweet man." She spoke the grateful, the hopeful, the openhearted truth. Moved, I could not help but wonder, could not help but imagine what it would be like if that gracious blessing were the last words my friend heard on this earth. How do you witness something like that and not be thankful, not be changed. It was benediction; out of the dark, clinical space, once again it seemed the Lord's face shone upon us.

*Charles Wesley in "Love Divine, All Loves Excelling"

Best Sermon of All

For it is God's will that by doing right you should put to silence the ignorance of foolish men.

1 Peter 2:15

Your actions speak so loudly, I cannot hear what you are saying.

-Ralph Waldo Emerson

Best sermon?
Best sermon is decency
Yes, decency, best sermon
Nothing else even close
Convincing apologetic?
Convincing apologetic is doing right
Yes, doing right, convinces
Nothing else even close
No matter how brilliant
How practiced proclaimer
How polished debater
No matter how orthodox
How pristine theological recitation
How fundamental academic dissertation
Regardless
It's example, good example
More profound than words
Most eloquent words
Best sermon of all.

So, don't speak God's love
Why bother while so mean
Don't preach welcome

Why bother while practitioners of privilege
While disciples of alienation
Remarkably disresembling Christ
The seeker till finding
Companioning least, most unlikely of these
Why bother while tone vindictive
While preferring judgment
Burdening the burdened
Don't bother while crushing the weak.

So, want to silence the foolish
So much noisy foolishness
Turn down volume, our volume, yes, ours
Empty ourselves, yes, you and me
Take form unpresuming, take form of servant
Then do
Do justice, love mercy, walk humbly
Fiercely loyal to right
Don't have to say a word
Not a single word
Just do
Best sermon of all.

Seen any good sermons lately?

Betrayed

"the Lord Jesus on the night he was betrayed took bread"
1 Corinthians 11:23

Which night, Lord?
You? Betrayed?
Which night would that be?

Was it night of silence, Lord?
Night I did not speak
Could not find my voice
Raise single word of protest
Was it that night?
Night fear, disrespect fouled the air
Vile rhetoric, weaponized rant
Dehumanizing positions
Self-serving policies
Trumpeted without embarrassment
Rationalized by your people
Defended using your name
While you labored becoming flesh
Risky, vulnerable, heart on the line
Cringing silence denied you
Cowardice endorsed evil
Sulking, ashamed, off into darkness
Was it that night Lord?

Or, was it night of expedience, Lord?
When playing it safe seemed smart
Compromise, calculating shrewdness
The better part of wisdom
I know what he said…
But can we tone it down a little?
Tell them what they want to hear
Wow them rather than scare them
After all he can be a little shrill

I know what he did…
But let's not be naïve, not impulsive
We need strategic planning
Goals, benchmarks, damage control
Can you spin murder on a cross?
This is cold, cruel world
Sunday morning far removed
Don't rock the boat
Now is not the right time
Reeking entangled complicity
Was it that night Lord?
Or, was it night of visitation, Lord?
Night you, reeling, smelly, you, uninvited
Night you stumbled into my way
Interfering, you, inconvenient
Sick, hungry, naked, you, imprisoned
Scrambling my tidy world
Addicted, bruised, filthy, you, lying
Seeking refuge among outcast
Close to brokenhearted
Sitting with crushed in spirit
And I…well, way too busy
Work important, too crucial to interrupt
Looking away, closing my heart
Who imagined, expected you there?
Was it that night, Lord?
There have been so many.

On the night he was betrayed, Jesus
The Lord Jesus took bread and broke it
Piece by crumbling piece
Given to dirty, blood-stained hands
Placed in desperate, thirsty mouths
Sustaining trembling, despairing souls
Lifting abused spirits
Though you wound me
Ignore me
Crucify me
Though you deny me over and over
Come to me

This is my body, even for you
Grace unspeakable to all betrayers
Every single one of us
Nothing separates from my love.

Bless Yourself

Jesus answered, "The first is, 'Hear, O Israel: The Lord our God, the Lord is one; and you shall love the Lord your God with all your heart, and with all your soul, and with all your mind, and with all your strength.' The second is this, 'You shall love your neighbor as yourself.' There is no other commandment greater than these."

Mark 12:29-31

Take care of yourself so you can take care of them. A bleeding heart is of no help to anybody if it bleeds to death.

-Frederick Buechner in TELLING SECRETS

Every year this simple, holy practice, this "Blessing of Hands," leaves me startled, chewing on some unexpected insight; consistently surprised by luminous, mysterious moments pondered for days. Wandering around blessing caregivers hands last Wednesday moved me more than ever. Perhaps part of the reason for my emotional response was it was our first "Blessing" since Corona upended our world. So we went out wondering, with new warnings and worries, with anxiety high, expectations low. You know the drill. Don't forget your mask. Keep your distance. Don't pull together large groups – maybe 2 or three at the most. And whatever your do, don't touch. Well, that last "thou shalt not" posed a bit of a challenge. Central to Hand Blessing has long been placing your oil soaked fingers in the palm of a colleague, making the sign of the cross, and while holding those precious hands praying, "May God bless the work of our hands." So, now what?

Leave it to Becky Dodson to come up with a creative work around on the touching prohibition. She purchased some small spray bottles we loaded up with baby oil. So we improvised, spraying the beautiful, healing hands our friends extended. By the end of the day I was a mess, not only covered with baby oil, but so filled with feeling, grateful, yet a little overwhelmed by what I witnessed. Like I wrote earlier, I was moved. I was moved when I walked up on that first unit at about 5:30am; lights dimmed, so quiet, so hushed, most every care giver in a patient room. It felt like walking into a sanctuary, though early, though still dark outside, the sacred work of healing faithfully attended. I was moved, voice catching, when we read the prayer together, over and over, the weary, hopeful voices appealing for renewal, daring to trust even after months and months of cautious strain, better days are coming. I was moved when I squirted the baby oil, spritzing hands and whispering the blessing, flooded with memories of trauma these brave souls face, frequently without appreciation. I was moved, and believe me a runny nose and tears are not easy to manage behind a mask with baby oil slick hands. But here is what I have been thinking about today. Quite often upon stretching their hands in my direction and receiving the spray of oil there was this look, this baffled, questioning look, "Now what in the world am I supposed to do with these dripping hands?" It was not long till it became part of the ritual itself. "I can't touch you," I explained. "So I am going to spray some baby oil on your hands and give you a blessing. Then rub your hands together and bless yourself."

Bless yourself. I am not sure there could be a better opportunity to relearn the truth – eventually, inevitably, we are absolutely no good to anyone else if we do not take care of ourselves - no better curriculum than this uneasy, sometimes terrifying, Pandemic year. Corona drove, and continues to drive home the message, whether we get it or not, self protection opens the door to protection of others; sometimes the difference between life and death. "Love your neighbor as you love yourself," Jesus taught. If you can't love yourself, nurture yourself, if you can't bless yourself, whatever you do for or to your neighbor will be more about your neediness, ultimately more about your agenda, than anything looking like the best interest of your neighbor. Bless yourself – nothing selfish, nothing strange, nothing shameful about it. In fact blessing yourself is the very foundation of healthy care giving. So, bless yourself. Bless your sacred, your precious self. Bless yourself, please. Your neighbor needs you to do it and so does this old, heaving world.

Bless the work of our hands, Lord
Renew our weary, our grieving spirits
Restore joy, reawaken gratitude
Remind, even on worst days
Remind, even in pandemic chaos
Remind, even there, we are never alone
For this is your work
Your sacred labor
You bless the work of our hands.
Amen.

Blessed Again by the Hurricane

Surely, he has borne our griefs and carried our sorrows.

Isaiah 53:4

"I picked him up in my arms and I carried him home."

-Wendell Berry in HANNAH COULTER

"I'm sorry Donna. Nikki called me. I'm sorry to hear Smitty's so sick." I was reaching out to my friend by phone, trying to provide comfort where little comfort can be found. "Thank you Reverend Dan. After all he's been through, now this. It's hard. It's just hard. This time you'd better light a big torch." And that determined, resilient soul, willing to exhaust herself to do anything for anyone in need, that warrior for the good, aptly named, "Hurricane Donna," one of the most unreasonably hopeful people I know, finally up against a problem she could not make better, finally stymied, crumbled, understandably lost her usual upbeat composure, and righteously grieved, sobbing as she tried to find breath to tell the rest of the story.

"You should have seen it, Reverend Dan. It was just like Baptist at the River. They knew we were on our way to the hospital. Guess who was there to meet us at the Emergency Room entrance...Dr. D! Can you believe that?" Donna was incredulous, her voice a mixture of sorrow and awe. "'No, we're not doing that,' he said. 'We're not waiting for any wheelchair.' And then you wouldn't believe it, Reverend Dan, Dr. D just opened the passenger door and picked Smitty up in his arms and carried him in. You should have seen it! It was just like Baptist at the River, just like old Baptist at the River!"

So much about this story is heartbreaking: Smitty ill, terribly ill, nearing the end of a long, dark slog, Donna helpless and afraid.

Donna's right, "It's hard. It's just hard." But there's more than desperate struggle here, there's also wonder, and surprisingly, some comfort as well; and though I didn't see this startling, this sacred moment, I'm guessing I can get pretty close, for I can imagine it, I can just imagine it. That big Texas cardiologist with the out-sized heart, that devoted, faithful brother in Christ, that compassion-filled healer, instinctively reaching down, gathering Smitty, holding him close, then carrying him, bearing him a little closer to home. It's what you do when you're family. Another incarnation, another visitation of the lasting spirit of "old Baptist at the River," and another reminder of our privilege of service, our call to bear one another's burdens.

Though tossed in the storm, though cruelly battered by terrifying chaos, though everything that can be shaken is shaken, some things do not change. For as always, Hurricane Donna, you help us remember - unselfconsciously bearing witness - for it's never about you, your generous life our example, you lead us toward our best selves.

Bonhoeffer in the Night

International Holocaust Remembrance Day

January 27, 2021

"Stretched out on my cot
I stare at the gray wall
I hear my own soul tremble and heave"
Dietrich Bonhoeffer in "Night Voices in Tegel"

"I've often found it a great help to think in the evening of all those who I know are praying for me."

Dietrich Bonhoeffer in LETTERS AND PAPERS FROM PRISON, Tegel, August 21, 1944

Imagine him resolute
Pictured strong, impressively brilliant
Decisive in light of day
Principled obstructor
Refusing to look away
Disdaining inaction's luxury
Risking security, abstaining safety
Till disrupting, derailing
Wrestling control from tyrant's hands
Imagine him defiant for justice
Battered, but bearing
Staggered, but lifting discipleship's cost
Till losing, till poured out one precious life
To the end, a wonder
To this day, lasting light
Yes, that's way imagined

Bright witness from darkness
Witness so bright.

But what of the night?
Night after heaving night
Night's gray, night's soul haunting silence
Save guards' withering threats
Save sufferers' terrified cries
Sleep escaping
Calm eroding
What of the night?
What accompanies there?
Merely regret? Only shame?
Badgering doubt? Unnerving lament?
Protest, bargaining, miserable longing?
What of the night?
What comforts, what sustains?
There in gray, soul haunting silence
Dramatic escape?
Miraculous rescue?
Promise of deeper devotion?
What comforts, what sustains?
Perhaps this
Perhaps gratitude
Yes, gratitude, resilient gratitude
Gratitude even there
Perhaps wonder
Yes, wonder, resilient wonder
Wonder even there
Perhaps blessing
Yes, blessing, resilient blessing
Blessing even there
Till remembering connected
By heart widely connected
Till recalling interceded
In prayer daily interceded
Hoping even from darkness

This deepest of darkness
Still waiting
Still watching
Still trembling for the morning
Witness, sturdy witness
Clear conscience in the night.

Bravest Frightened Person I Know

Even there your hand will guide me, your right hand will hold me fast.

Psalm 139:10

I have a lot of faith and a lot of fear a lot of the time.

-Anne Lamott in "Small Victories"

"If you are going to give me bad news, you have to hold my hand." Amy repeatedly learned the hard way and her wary greeting bore witness. Struggling with ovarian cancer, Amy slugged through more bad news than anyone should have to deal with. She endured surgery, radiation, chemotherapy, desperate trips to the hospital, day after endlessly long day of not knowing, anxious, terrified waiting, and in-patient confinement.

Some of us had the blessing of walking alongside Amy for much of that time. I am confident I will be learning from Amy and recalling reasons to be grateful for her my whole life. I think of her on a regular basis. I remember Amy whenever a patient reluctantly admits they are afraid, as if anxiety and fear of life and death ordeals of the hospital are shameful signs of spiritual weakness and failure. Somewhere along the line, too many sincere people of faith have been sold an overly simplistic and false formula - something like this - the more faith, the less fear. So, instead of finding comfort in faith when confronted with dark, nerve-wracking uncertainty, many are embarrassed, or believe they are disappointing God because they can no longer pretend they are not afraid.

Amy showed us a better way. I learned to think of her as the bravest frightened person I have known. Her disease and its treatment horrified her. She was so spooked, just the sight of the hospital building made her physically ill. But month after month, year after year, Amy kept pushing ahead and, in her stumbling, resolute journey made it possible for us to experience a new definition of courage.

51

Amy still helps me remember courage is not not being afraid. Instead, Amy modeled courage as honestly speaking up, asking for what you need, and walking on, even while it makes all kinds of sense to be afraid.

Among Amy's many gifts is one lasting image continuing to stir my imagination, challenging superficial presumptions about what it means to live with faith. I hear it in her surprising, brave request when her doctor walked into her hospital room holding dreaded test results. "If you are going to give me bad news, you have to hold my hand." Amy helped me see faith in the thick of threats and uncertainty does not mean I am always heroic, at peace, and unafraid. Faith does not mean hiding my anxiety behind spiritual bluster. Instead, faith means summoning trust even when I am afraid; even when I am up against a challenge bigger than I am. Faith is trusting there is One always ready to hold my hand, understanding how overwhelmed and weak I feel. Amy's trembling, welcoming grasp is a sacred sign, a defiant witness no matter how difficult the news might be, I am not alone, God's right hand still holds me fast, will never let me go.

Breaking the Rules

The church knows all the rules. But it doesn't know what goes on in a single human heart.

-Graham Greene in THE HEART OF THE MATTER

And Jesus, moved with compassion, troubled, indignant, stretched out his hand and touched the man, saying, "I will. Be clean."
Mark 1:41

What was he doing there?
Publicly prostrate
What was he doing there?
There, rather than conforming
There, rather than banished
Shamefully sequestered
Driven from public space
Not to mention temple
Not to mention God
But there he was
There, out in open
Filled with irrepressible protest
Pleading, bargaining, daring
Nothing to lose
Abject rebellion, damning rules
Rejecting acceptable conduct
Demanding inclusion
If you will, if you really want to
If you will, you can do it
You can make me clean
No longer squelching desperation
No longer silent
Seizing moment
Dangerous, hope-filled moment
If you will…

And everyone held breath
Leering, curious
Ready, so ready with judgment
What would he do?
Why, "right thing," of course
Jesus always does "right thing"
Condemn the man
Clear the square
Summon National Guard
Call him what he is
Why, he 's unclean
Vermin, mere animal
Unfit acknowledgment
For company with decent people
That's "right thing"
Law and Order thing
That's what rules say
Be gone! Get away!
Crawl back in nearest hole
Back where you belong
Back outside walls
Clearly, what Jesus will do
He will do "right thing."

Or…maybe not
Definitely not this radical
Not this unpredictable
Not this rabble-rousing Rabbi
Slowly stretching out his hand
Oh, he knows the rules
But now he's beyond reason
Troubled, indignant
Now he's mad
Yes, Jesus mad, thoroughly disgusted
Now driven by compassion
Now dismisses "right thing"
Breaking rules
Breaking rules not from ignorance
Breaking rules because offended
Rules glorying self-righteousness

Rules demeaning
Spirit eroding, deadly rules
Stretching out his hand
Blessing connection
Rejecting division
Consciously, intentionally
Stretching out his hand
Valuing person over commandment
Humiliated soul over orthodoxy
Dignity over purity
Abundance over legalism
Mercy over judgment
Always, always over judgment.

Courageously, sacrificially
With full knowledge of scandal
Enraging pious
Threatening powerful
Raising execution's specter
Broken-hearted Jesus
Stretching out his hand
Reckless, regardless risk
Oblivious to condemnation
Consequence dismissed
Spirit of Lord upon him
Jesus breaks the rules.

Still on the loose?
Tearing down walls?
Eating with sinners?
Welcoming despised?
Challenging intolerance?
Laboring to make us whole?
Disgusted Jesus
Still breaking the rules?
I think so, I hope so
What dangerous
What necessary
What wondrous love is this?

But Jesus Saw

He was despised and rejected by men;
* a man of sorrows, and acquainted with grief;*
and as one from whom men hide their faces
* he was despised, and we esteemed him not.*
Surely he has borne our griefs
* and carried our sorrows,*
yet we esteemed him stricken,
* smitten by God, and afflicted.*
But he was wounded for our transgressions,
* he was bruised for our iniquities;*
upon him was the chastisement that made us whole,
* and with his stripes we are healed.*
Isaiah 53:3-5

"The trick is to think of some way for them to have their fun without beating you up."

James Baldwin in "This Morning, This Evening, So Soon"

Never saw "The Passion of Christ"
Guess could've gone, closed my eyes
Guess could've gone, looked away
Why, if Jesus endured brutality for you
Why, least you could bear witness
But never saw "The Passion of Christ"
Violence, violence, saturating violence
Knew broken heart
Weary, broken heart could not stand it.

Will not view Tyre's beating
Guess could try, close my eyes
Guess could try, look away
Why, if Tyre endured evil's onslaught

Why, least you could bear witness
But will not view Tyre's murder
Violence, violence, saturating violence
Know broken heart
Weary, broken heart cannot stand it
Cannot stand one more horror
One more needlessly battered soul
One more raging outcry
One more wailing through empty night
Cannot stand one more demand for change ignored
Mocking evidence intractable corruption
Will not view Tyre's murder
Violence, violence, saturating violence
Know broken heart
Weary broken heart cannot stand it.

But Jesus saw, hope Jesus saw
Trust, never closing eyes
Saw, never looking away
But Jesus saw, hope Jesus saw
Driven down street's grinding filth
Soaked, pooling life's precious blood
But Jesus saw, hope Jesus saw
Stalked, tortured, preyed by merciless
Betrayed, heartless gloating, left to die
But Jesus saw, hope Jesus saw
Held till breathed excruciating last
Understanding's weight, compassion's burden
But Jesus saw, hope Jesus saw
Compelling tenderness, tending tears
Gently, so gently, Jesus draws near
Receives, lifts, Jesus carries
Sorrow bearing, like so many
Far too many, his shattered children
Accompanies Tyre till safely home.

Keep watch Lord Jesus, keep watch

See what we cannot see
What we refuse to see
Comfort grieving
Heal fractured, fearful world
Make new bewildered hearts
Over and over, we know not what we do.

Careful Attention

"So, could you not watch with me one hour?"

Matthew 26:40

"Healing means, first of all, the creation of an empty but friendly space where those who suffer can tell their story to someone who can listen with real attention."

-Henri Nouwen in REACHING OUT

The family was gone and who could blame them. After months of serious illness, numerous, frantic, anxious trips to the hospital, hour after hour of uncertain, even terrifying, waiting, concluded by a couple weeks' stay in the alien land of an Intensive Care Unit, they were grief-stricken, emotionally and physically exhausted. Bearing witness to their great love, they were present, always present, right there, through the worst, staying by their patient's side even while she was extubated, there when she took her last breath, gathered their things, held on to each other, and walked away. After saying good-by, I went back to the unit because I wanted to thank the nurse, one of the best. He had been exceptional in his care of the patient and the folks who loved her. When I got to the room, the door and blinds were closed. Thinking he was probably doing some last minute things, preparing the body for transfer to the funeral home, I tapped on the door. The next few minutes astonished and moved me. I am confident I will never forget them.

I have been a hospital chaplain for a long time. I should know better than to assume I have seen it all, but sometimes I get in a rut; even this intense place, often filled with chaos, begins to feel routine. I simply was not ready for what I walked in on, what I was invited into, that sacred morning during Holy Week a few days ago. But I will be thinking about it for a long time, grateful for the necessary reminders it holds. When the nurse opened the door and I began to thank him, I realized he was not alone. Three of his colleagues, his fellow nurses, were with him. After shutting the door, he sat down beside the patient's bed and took her hand. "We did not want her to die alone," he said softly. Although initially a little confused, it became clear to me, even though the patient stopped breathing, her heart continued beating for a few more minutes. And during that time, that careful, holy time, this company of attentive compassion drew close, surrounding her, and though she was unaware of it, held her hand. She was not alone.

This has been a maddening and strange week for nurses. A mouthy politician took some ignorant and cheap shots at their expense and the fallout has thundered through social media and network news. Too bad Washington State Senator Maureen Walsh could not have been with me the other morning rather than playing to the cameras trying to score political points. It would have done her some good; she could have seen what I saw from a front row seat the kind of care nurses often provide when there really seems to be nothing else they can do. Every one of those folks in the room was terribly busy, highly trained, accustomed to being responsible for multiple clinical procedures during any one shift, calling for skill, accurate judgment, and sometimes aggressive intervention. Nursing is the toughest work I have ever witnessed up close on a day to day basis. If it is not a calling, you are not going to last as a nurse, you just aren't. And that calling often extends beyond cure to the costly vulnerability of helpless, human connection. In that space last week, from my perspective on the edge, I encountered four people setting aside the tyranny of mere productivity, as important as reasonable staffing expectations might be; I saw them resisting pressing agendas and intentionally deciding to treat this person, this patient, just like they would want their family member cared for at such a moment; that the intervention called for was respectful, whole-hearted, presence. And that's exactly what they did, attending quietly till the end; the very end; till the last heartbeat. It seems trite to say it this way, but it was an honor to be there, a privilege to witness commitment to healing at its best.

Carried

*And when Jesus saw their faith, he said to the paralytic,
"My son your sins are forgiven."*

Mark 2:5

"Often in a church I have thought while there is
scant hope for me, I can ask God to strengthen the
holiness of all these good people here – that man,
that woman, child...and I do so. In St. Anne's
Basilica it struck me in the middle of a white-robed
priest's French service that possibly everybody in
that stone chamber, and possibly everybody in
every other house of prayer on earth, thinks this
way. What if we are all praying for one another in
the hope that the others are holy, when we are not?
Of course this must be the case. Then – again
possibly – surely it adds up to something or other?"

-Annie Dillard in FOR THE TIME BEING

"Everybody needs help sometime."

-Brent Thomas, Community Resource Coordinator
at Carolina Village

"The way we are, we are members of each other.
All of us. Everything. The difference ain't in who
is a member and who is not, but who knows it and
who don't."

Wendell Berry in WILD BIRDS

I am a "carrier." Carrier is my preferred identity, my most
comfortable and meaningful function. I began to learn that at 22
years of age, just weeks from entering the seminary, helping my frail,
tiny friend Juanita carry her dying husband, Buck, to another room

in the house. It was startling, we struggled, grasping, slipping, almost dropping his helpless weight, nearly overwhelmed. Forty seven years have passed and I still remember the frightening strain, yet, also moved with lasting, profound gratification for those few difficult minutes of carrying, holding, helping. I am sure I will never forget. It is not too dramatic to claim, that experience with those two exhausted, elderly souls was one of the key formative moments for me in ministry. I am a helper. I am a carrier.

But sometimes - and in recent weeks it has become uncomfortably clear – sometimes, despite my stubborn independence, sometimes my strength, my capacity to control, or even partially manage life's constant chaos is not enough - sometimes I need to be carried. As Brent Thomas reminded several months ago, "Dan, everybody needs help sometime." And this time of rattling disruption has been my time. But in ways I could not have imagined, from places and circumstances, and from folks I could not have anticipated, the steadying help has come – opening doors and windows, quiet, encouraging conversations over coffee, quick messages and notes and lunches and prayer – all have helped me find my footing - all have proven to be reminders I have been and am being carried - like Buck, thoroughly and maddeningly, dependent and vulnerable, but still held and blessed – learning, even against my will, when I am weak, I am strong, carried through harrowing dark by so many of you, incarnations of the abiding, the sufficient grace of God.

A late night text of providential, of impeccable timing - a welcoming, mercy-filled, an Epiphany of a text - filled with indescribably good news, revealing a way forward, penetrated my anxious obsessing last night and I awakened to this rainy morning knowing again, knowing perhaps more deeply than ever, yes, I am carried, I am accompanied. No matter what challenges this day holds, I am surrounded, borne by the faithfulness of others, a grateful witness "light shines in the darkness, and the darkness comprehendeth it not." Trust grows the darkness never will.

Catchers

If anyone would be first, he must be last of all and servant of all

Mark 9:35

What a moment; Dodger legends Sandy Koufax, in his 80's, and Don Newcomb, in his 90's, throwing out the first pitch before the Seventh Game of the World Series last night. It is unacceptable to me that those two fantastic pitchers could be so old when it seems they were on the mound just yesterday. Still, it brought a smile to my face. Baseball, the greatest sport, is sentimental in that way. But that was not the only reason I was smiling and shaking my head. I was reliving a memory 54 years old. Sometime in the first few minutes following the conclusion of the 1963 World Series I did one of the more foolish things I had done up to that point in my young life. I flushed my 1960 Sandy Koufax rookie baseball card. Well, actually I tore the card up into tiny pieces and then flushed it. I see that card at most shows today or on eBay with a price tag of several hundred dollars pasted on the front. Now that was an expensive piece of vengeance. It is an embarrassing thing to confess, but if you were a New York Yankee fan in 1963, you probably understand. In my ten-year-old mind Sandy Koufax, the great Dodger pitcher who dominated the Yankee hitters, was the worst of villains. I held him personally responsible for the Yankees' humiliating defeat. No self-respecting Yankee fan would hold on to a Koufax card; it was a matter of integrity.

It has taken a while, but now I know flushing all that money down the toilet was not my only piece of mistaken thinking. Saint Paul reminds me of that when he writes, "For the body does not consist of one member, but of many." Paul did not know anything about baseball, but he sure knew a lot about mutual respect, healthy dependency and the cooperation it takes to accomplish most of the important tasks in life. In fact, the picture Paul describes of the church being like a body without any unessential parts, a body where every member has dignity and an important contribution to make, sounds like a good image for the complex activity I witness every day in the hospital. I am constantly reminded if I am going to do my work well, I need the help of colleagues in multiple disciplines. It is an over-used phrase, but it is true, "we are all in this together," or listening to the words of Paul again, "If one member suffers, all suffer together; if one member is honored, all rejoice together."

I suppose it is only normal to focus on the superstar. Sandy Koufax was a fantastic pitcher, one of the best ever. But as Max Depree reminds us in <u>Leadership is an Art</u>, there is one way to turn even Sandy Koufax into a terrible pitcher. That almost unimaginable feat could be accomplished by letting one of us, by letting me, be his catcher. So, do you remember who the Dodger catcher was during the 1963 World Series? I guess I should have flushed John Roseboro.

Caught in the Light

"I am an ignorant pilgrim, crossing a dark valley. And yet for a long time, looking back, I have been unable to shake off the feeling that I have been led."

-Wendell Berry in JAYBER CROW

I could hear the phone demanding attention way back in the dark church office. But I was on my way out the door into the cold Ohio night, headed home and for a moment tempted to just let the thing ring. Reluctantly, I went back, stumbling through the shadowy building, while the phone kept up its insistent racket till I finally found it and answered. "Hello, Dan this is Maurice Briggs down in Winston-Salem. I am calling on behalf of my church. We are looking for a Minister of Youth and someone gave us your name." I was stunned, and once I found my bearings, thanked Maurice, telling him as much as I appreciated his interest, and felt honored a church like Knollwood would consider me, I believed my next place of ministry would not be with youth. And that really could have been the end of the conversation. Who would have been surprised if we said our goodbyes and I would never hear of Maurice Briggs again. But for some reason Maurice hung in there, asking the question opening space to disclose a dream. "Then where do you see yourself in ministry?" I told him I just finished two units of clinical training and felt led toward hospital ministry, probably the first time I dared put it into words. And without missing even a beat, Maurice shocked me for the second time in five minutes. "Well, Dan, I am a CPE supervisor in the School of Pastoral Care at North Carolina Baptist Hospital and we are still receiving applications for next year's residents group. Are you interested?" Wonder. Even to this very day, unshakeable wonder. Sometimes I still imagine hearing that phone ringing way off in the distance and shutter realizing how close I came to just ignoring it. And as for Maurice, I would soon learn his patient attention on the phone was not out of character, and that unlikely exchange would not be the last time I was recipient of his gift for listening carefully, then asking just the right question. Light bearer.

Fits and starts
Hints and surprises
Near accidental as accidental can be
Make of it
Call it what you will
Spirit's prompting?
Fortunate, very fortunate timing?
Plain, unapologetic, good luck?
Make of it
Call it what you will
Unintentional recipient
Unforeseen blessing
Call it incomprehensible
Passing epiphany
Unexpected revelation
Make of it
Call it what you will
I call it caught
Call it startled by the light
Why, I call it persistent grace
Looking back, all the difference
Without it could not see at all.

Deep-ended

Out of the depths I cry to thee, O God.
Psalm 130:1

"I think there is no suffering greater than by the doubts of those who want to believe. I know what torment this is, but can only see it, in myself anyway, as the process by which faith is deepened."
Flannery O'Connor

My friend, Mark, shared the quote you see above from the brilliant often troubling writer, Flannery O'Connor, on social media. It's wonderful, I believe so very true, and I'm stealing it, grateful not only for its honesty, but also indebted because Mark has given me a new word. He didn't mean to, and I "doubt" it's even a real word, but it's inspired, and I'm pretty sure it's going to be working on me for a while. The word is "deep-ended," or as Mark shared, "deepended," mistakenly adding a "d" to "deepened" in O'Connor's quote.

Who can't identify with the experience of being deep-ended - kicked out into the dark, howling waves by some booger we never saw coming, totally disoriented, suddenly treading water way, way over our heads - desperately trying to make sense out of a harrowing place we never meant to be. I know I can. Sooner or later, most of us learn what it's like to be deep-ended, wondering and questioning if our old sources of security and faith still hold.

It seems doubt has too long been a shame-filled word in the spiritual life, and the price has been painfully high, resulting in a great deal of pretended certainty, mistrust, and lonely secrecy. I love O'Connor's vulnerable effort to rehab the old, uncomfortable, very familiar struggle. Reminds me of my absolute favorite word on doubt - it's from Frederick Buechner and can be found in his insightful little book, WISHFUL THINKING:

"Whether your faith is that there is a God or that there is not a God, if you don't have any doubts, you are either kidding yourself or asleep. Doubts are the ants in the pants of faith. They keep it awake and moving."

I remember the moment I encountered this proclamation of good news by Buechner. I was a student at the seminary a hundred years ago and I had a doubt or two. In fact, challenged in the classroom, maddening doubt seemed to thrive. But Buechner's take on doubt was like a revelation. I felt spoken for, more hopeful, and sometimes, as Buechner's daring imagination still accompanies, and continues to hook my attention, I even feel a little more brave.

Welcome to the deep-end. Eventually we find ourselves here. Might as well join the rest of us and jump in. We are not alone.

Dissent: Patriotic Practice

Silence in the face of evil is itself evil
God will not hold us guiltless
Not to speak is to speak
Not to act is to act.
Dietrich Bonhoeffer

From its colonial origins, the United States has often been the land
of the free and the home of the dissenter. In 2020, the voice of
dissent may be freedom's last hope. Clearly the rule of law and the
Golden Rule are under threat among us. Silence now anticipates a
time when silence may be mandated by principalities and powers.
Bill Leonard in "Lent 2020: Improvising grace and embracing
repentance, civility and dissent in 'a time of national urgency'"
From Baptist News Global, February 27, 2020

Love it or leave it?
If all you do's complain
If you're so unhappy
Griping, opposing
Fussing, fulminating
Love it or leave it
Just go back
Back where you came from
Back to broken, corrupt
Back to hell holes
Just love it
Love it like I do
Blind, zealous
Dripping with self-interest
Empty of criticism, absent dissent
Just love it or leave.

Did you hear that Jackie Robinson?
How 'bout you Martin Luther King?
Were you listening Susan Anthony?
Then Stonewall

Then Little Rock, then Birmingham
Not to mention Henry, Jefferson
John Woolman, Clarence Jordan
RUTH BADER GINSBURG
And Sojourner Truth, yes, Sojourner Truth
And on and on
Great cloud determined faithful
Unwilling to wait, refusing to comply
No longer silent
Laying down life for change
What were you thinking?
How dare you complain?
Just love it or leave.

In nation birthed by protest
Patriotism fired by dissent
Citizenship debated, defined, refined
Then refined again by free speech
Courageously holding variant opinion
Essential role of loyal opposition
More passionate
More honest than mere acquiescence
In nation unfinished
Challenged, yet, by diversity enriched
Still building, still exploring
Still understanding, still uncovering
Still forming more perfect union
How do you love an idea like that?
Embrace wild soul of freedom like that?

Daunting, near impossible
But ours the work to do
Ours to bear witness
Ours to live out
Could it mean quarreling, advocating
Listening, compromising, mending
Learning as we go
Could it mean objecting, criticizing
Maddening contrariness
Perhaps dissent

Could it mean fighting, insisting
Crying out for something better
Something more humane
More respectful
More inclusive
More humble
More decent
More consistent with liberty's dream
Could it be this messy project takes us all?
Love it that way
Find voice and love it that way
Don't go anywhere
Love it and stay
Every single
Every dissenting one of us.

Don't Know Why

But the Lord God called to the man, and said to him, "Where are you?"

Genesis 3:9

"God is somewhere other than the place we think to look."

Lauren Winner in STILL

God shows up where God shows up
We don't know why
God shows up where God shows up
So, we wait, then while waiting watch
So, we watch, then while watching listen.

God shows up where God shows up
We don't know why
So, abandon anxious perfectionism
Shred creedal formulas
Reject charts, cease obsessing timelines
Push exacting
Push fill in the blank
Push limiting, confining
Push simplifying
Toss one correct answers aside.

God shows up where God shows up
We don't know why
God shows up, startles, then scatters
Liberates fear-filled certainty
God show's up, the answer's "Yes"
God brave, God wholehearted
God's answer's "Yes"

Too wide, too deep
Irreducible, yes, incomprehensible
Defying limit, overwhelming any blank
God's answer, mysterious
God's answer always "Yes."
Unrestrained, God answers, "Yes.

God shows up where God shows up
We don't know why
Take off your shoes, yes, take off your shoes
Anywhere, yes, anywhere's holy ground.

Dreaming Beyond a Shattered Dream

*May those who sow in tears reap with shouts of joy! He that
goes forth weeping, bearing the seed for sowing, shall come
home with shouts of joy, bringing his sheaves with him.*

Psalm 126:4-6

For almost 20 years at old Baptist Hospital the first thing I did most
mornings was meet with Paul, RN and House Supervisor. Paul
claimed those early morning rounds were part of my continuing
education. There are some things you just do not learn in seminary.
I am sure if I was effective as a chaplain, a great deal of the credit
goes to Paul. Ostensibly, we met so he could bring me up to speed
about how things had been through the night in the hospital; to see
what the chaplains needed to follow up on. That usually happened,
but the fun was to hear the most recent jokes and stories and to
complain about the Braves. Paul had an endless supply of
foolishness and wisdom and on particularly difficult mornings,
mornings of confusion, and sometimes shock, he liked to quote that
great philosopher Mike Tyson. It seems in a pre-fight press
conference, then heavy-weight champion Mike Tyson was asked
about his opponent's boast; his claim he could beat Tyson because
he had a plan. To which Tyson replied, "Everybody has a plan until
they get hit." Paul loved that story. Every time I heard him tell it, it
seemed so true. I am sure I will be using Paul's material my whole
life; at least some of it.

For all his dreamy, triumphant language, the author of Psalm 126
was facing one of the most daunting spiritual tasks that can come
our way. The challenge of finding the spiritual courage to dream
beyond a shattered dream. Many who find themselves in this
building are better acquainted with this dark and difficult spot than
any would like to be. Most of us can muster the daring and
excitement to dream the first time. But what about after the
miscarriage, or the reoccurrence, or the divorce, or the relapse, or

the redeployment, or the downsizing, or some other crushing blow? Can you still dream, can you still hope there? Sometimes, I am not sure I can. I am always amazed by and grateful for the people I encounter who with a stubborn faith and resiliency find a way to stand back up and move ahead. They are our spiritual teachers. They keep getting back in the ring with Mike Tyson. "Our real calling," writes Craig Barnes, "is to discern what we will do after what we thought should happen, doesn't happen."

Dreaming beyond, trusting beyond, hoping beyond, working beyond a shattered dream. That was the task before the Psalmist and part of what challenges me as I listen to him take it on is how realistic he was. He seems to know what he was hoping for in the midst of his tears and grief was absolutely impossible, impossible apart from the restoring grace of God. As I overhear his commitment to persevere, I get the impression it was not just his outward circumstances he was asking God to renew, but his longing heart as well – his joy. And that really is God's work – God's part. Our work, our part, is to endure. Not a very fun word, but endurance takes the next step when what you thought should happen, doesn't happen. Endurance keeps the door of hope open, watching for the dawn through long difficult night.

Eating Before Hunger

All the way home and through the evening, I kept chewing on it, ruminating about a conversation with a patient; really a conversation with a friend who happened to be a patient. A friend who up till a few weeks ago was going strong, enjoying his life, especially, his family and his work. A friend who suddenly is grappling with making sense out of a devastating diagnosis putting him on his back, totally dependent, and probably with limited time. So, when I sat with him last week, we did not do our usual battle about ACC Basketball. Instead, we talked about something which is next to impossible for us to do. We talked about learning to give up control. And as challenging as that conversation was; as threatening as it is for me to put myself in my friend's place, what I had a difficult time shaking, what almost haunted me yet encouraged me, was his baffled reflection on a decision he made a few years before; a decision he made almost without thinking to become a part of a weekly Bible study. And now in this moment of crisis, it was clear my friend was drawing on that well of spiritual nurture the Bible study and the relationships tended there placed in his life. He was amazed he had even been led to go, and now was amazed at how much he really needed and benefited from it. That seemingly, almost casual decision had become a lifeline.

The world of wisdom and advice is filled with truisms; one line zingers that mostly simplify and fail to honor how wonderfully rich and complex life can be. As shaky as they are, combine a truism with religion and often you not only have bad theology, but they are given more credibility than they deserve. You've heard them before. "God helps those who help themselves." Or, "God never puts more on us than we can bear." It would not be difficult to find those who insist those two are in the Bible. While recognizing truisms are treacherous territory, a couple came to mind as I thought about my friend. They seem to go in opposite directions. The first one; "experience is something you get about 5 minutes after you really need it." And the other comes from my grandfather who enjoyed joking, "I am not really hungry, but I am going to go ahead and eat anyway because that way when I get hungry, I will have already eaten." Think about that one, chew on that one, for a few minutes.

Life has a way of teaching us, or giving us the opportunity to learn, there really is no way to be ready for everything. Plan as carefully as you can, there is still something coming your way you could never imagine, something you could not be prepared for. However, listening to my friend the other day, and listening to Jesus, helped me realize there is something to be said for spiritual preparation. I hear it in my friend's wonder about his years in Bible study, and I hear it in that intimidating, yet comforting prayer from Jesus on the cross, "Father, into thy hands;" a prayer of surrender and trust. Probably most everyone knows those words are not original to Jesus; they can be found in Psalm 31. Jesus, in that moment of spiritual and physical pain reached deep into the well of spiritual practice to pray a prayer every little Jewish girl and boy recited before they went to sleep. Could a child ever be prepared for this day of brutality? Could that little boy imagine a terrible moment like this? Could he know this simple statement of trust taught by his mother, this short memorized child's prayer, would remind him he was not alone in the most godforsaken time of his life?

Maybe my grandfather was on to something in his absurd statement about eating before you get hungry. The foundation for surrender, the nurturing of trust; the time to learn where the hand holds are and who it is who holds our hand in the darkness; all of that is best done before the storm hammers home. I heard that from a friend last week and I think it is true.

Enduring the Night

When I lie down I say, "When shall I arise?" But the night is long, and I am full of tossing till dawn. Job 7:4

"I should tell how my grim experiences often follow me into the night, and the only way I can shake them off is by reciting one hymn after another and that when I wake up it is generally with a sigh, rather than with a hymn of praise."
Dietrich Bonhoeffer in LETTERS AND PAPERS FROM PRISON

I am awake, Lord, wide awake
Long before wanted to be
Before hoped
Before meant to be
Exposed, so edgy, so aggravated
Assaulted by every anxiety
Every impossible concern
Every well buried secret
Rising up, pushing in, gathering round
Collecting dues.

I am awake, Lord, wide awake
Long before wanted to be
Before hoped
Before meant to be
Out of depths sighing, crying out to you
For here in dark, you are lone listener
Here in dark, few illusions, little to lose
Here in dark, know more than I wish
Even with all my planning, life's uncertain
With all my justification, consequence mocks
With all my worry, those I love still at risk
With all my denial, days pass quickly, mostly gone

With all my belligerence
All my clinging defensiveness, security illusive
For here in dark, wisdom rises as well
There is no frantic busyness
No distraction, no escaping daunting demands.

I am awake, Lord, wide awake
Long before wanted to be
Before hoped
Before meant to be
Yet, beneath empty striving
Quiet, yet, stubbornly insistent
Urging through, then above anxious noise
Still, small, patiently reaching, now listen
Inhabiting darkness, listen
Hope's persistent whisper, keep listening
Hear, calling, seeking, still seeking
Emmanuel, approaching
Emmanuel, alongside
Emmanuel, abiding
Can it be, bravest longing?
Can it be, Emmanuel, with us?

"Listen, listen deeply, then deeper still
Listen, you are not alone
There's no wakefulness
No matter how fitful, regardless how maddening
No wakefulness I am not present
Bending low, I accompany
Tossing, brooding, I labor with you
Bear burdens of struggling night
Lifting, I carry toward dawn."

Enslaved

'Lo, these many years I have served you, and I never disobeyed your command; yet you never gave me a kid, that I might make merry with my friends. But when this son of yours came, who has devoured your living with harlots, you killed for him the fatted calf!'

Luke 15:29-30

"It was the kind of thing only his father would forgive him for."

Marilynne Robinson in GILEAD

What if
He'd seen enough
He'd seen too much
Every heart, no matter how open
Every heart has a limit
He'd stood bewildered
He'd stood helplessly by
Every spirit no matter how resilient
Every last spirit eventually dies.

What if
He'd hoped
Sometimes hoped against hope
He'd hoped something better
Hoped till could hope no longer
Hoped till remarkable perseverance
Till duty's stalwart allegiance
Till steady, till quiet trustworthiness
Hoped till that stream slowly ran dry.

What if
He'd tolerated enough
He'd tolerated too much
Too much callous self-absorption
Too much wasting, reckless privilege
He'd dried beloveds' desperate tears
Waited betrayed, fearing worst
Waited long, through harrowing night.

What if
He'd heard enough
He'd heard too much
Heard numerous half-hearted apologies
Myriad fanciful, such creative excuses
Too many ruined promises to believe again
Ever believe again.

What if
Now, burdened
Now heartsick, now wounded
Tragically enslaved, by resentment bound
Now defended, so well defended
Now unmovable, bears heart of stone
Now begrudging, dismissively sneers
"This son of yours
This enabled
This narcissistic
This entitled
This son of yours means nothing
Will never mean anything to me."

What if
He'd seen enough
He'd seen too much he wouldn't
Couldn't forgive, couldn't unsee
Damaged, he damages
He breaks his father's heart.

Every Breath

"This is what I know: that the small is huge, that the tiny is vast, that pain is part and parcel of the gift of joy, and that this is love, and then there is everything else. You either walk toward love or away from it with every breath you draw."
Brian Doyle in "The Final Frontier"

Love never ends...
1 Corinthians 13:8

Tell me, I asked
Tell me about her
And so he did
Though grieving, generous in telling
Though strangers, opened his heart
His grateful, his ancient
Quietly opened struggling heart
Slowly, carefully, from beginning
"She was just an 18 year old girl."

Oh
Oh this, pay attention, pay attention
Yes this, surpassing mere data
More, much more, transcending history
This glimpse
This mystery
This, sacred revelation
Witness of lifetime
Love palpable
Love stronger
Love outlasting even death.
Tell me, I asked
Tell me about her
And so he did

"She was just an 18 year old girl."

Always will be
Always will be.

Every Day is Mother's Day

His mother seems to know him the way all mothers know their children: her body remembers his.

Richard Lischer in STATIONS OF THE HEART

Hazel died late one Easter Sunday. She just got sick so quickly and before we could even realize it, she was gone. A couple days later, I stood with her two sisters, Ethel and Cleo. We gathered in their mother's room at the nursing home. It was the morning of the funeral and it seemed to make some sense to spend time with their mother, Sara. Sara was 103 years old. Although her mind was keen and bright, her old body was frail and weak, just worn out. Now, enduring what has to be one of parenting's most difficult, most impossible tasks, grappling the death of a child. Sarah was not going to be able to attend Hazel's service – she was just too frail.

I cannot describe to you the kind of joy that had been a part of most of my conversations with Sara. She loved her church. She always had someone read the church newsletter to her and the bulletin. She constantly asked me about those who were sick and in the hospital. She told wonderful ancient stories. One of her favorites being the day some 90 years earlier she was baptized in the Yadkin River with the whole church gathered on the bank. Visiting Sara was never a pastoral task, it was spiritual sustenance. However, on the morning of Hazel's funeral, I wanted to be most anywhere else except in Sara's room. But once again, she surprised me. After several minutes of quiet, sobbing, grief, and my clumsy attempts to provide some kind of comfort, she looked up from her bed at her daughter, then in her seventies, and said, "Ethel, you know how easy it is for you to catch cold. When you are out in the cemetery this morning, you make sure you have your coat on." Touched deeply, I remember thinking, "Once a mother, always a mother." That risky, holy labor, like love itself, is never done. As a member of the human race who will never be a mother, standing in the sacred warmth of that moment, I was, still am, amazed, will always be in awe.

Everybody

And when Jesus saw their faith, he said to the paralytic, "My son your sins are forgiven."

Mark 2:5

"I start to suspect that the reason my Christian life hasn't completely conked out is that even when I am not praying, other people pray for me, on my behalf."

Lauren Winner in STILL

Which of these three, do you think, proved neighbor to the man who fell among the robbers?" He said, "The one who showed mercy on him." And Jesus said to him, "Go and do likewise."

Luke 10:36-37

"If two neighbors know that they may seriously disagree, but that either of them, given even a small change of circumstances may desperately need the other, should they not keep between them a sort of prepaid forgiveness? They ought to keep it ready to hand, like a fire extinguisher, in case it may prove useful."

Wendell Berry in THE NEED TO BE WHOLE

"Everybody needs help some time, Dan."

Brent Thomas, Community Resource Coordinator at Carolina Village

Everybody needs help some time
Everybody
Everybody needs help some time
Do you believe that?
Imagine it in middle of the night?

Everybody needs help some time
Everybody
Sounds weak, sounds clingy, so clingy
Dependent, why, sounds un-American
For we value autonomy
Admire self-sufficiency
Our faith, competition
Our security, acquisition
Our trust, "free" markets
You tend your business, I'll tend mine.

But, everybody needs help some time
Everybody
Everybody needs help some time
Do you believe that?
Imagine it in middle of the night?
If you don't, just wait
If you don't, you will
One day, inevitable
One day, inescapable
No matter wealth, even awash in resource
No matter power, even unreasonably determined
No matter, one day you will
You'll need some compassion
One day, you'll need to be neighbored.

Everybody needs help some time
Everybody.

Exception

We are afflicted in every way, but not crushed.

2 Corinthians 4:8

"The way we are, we are members of each other.
All of us. Everything. The difference ain't in who
is a member and who is not, but who knows it and
who don't."

Wendell Berry in WILD BIRDS

"The relentlessness of tragedy is redeemed by the
persistence of grace."

Wendell Berry in WHAT ARE PEOPLE FOR

I'm not the exception, no, not the exception
There's no immunity, no immunity at all
No special privilege, no self-serving entitlement
No personal deal
Raise outrageous case, I can rouse defenders
Demonize opposition, charade victimization
Inflamed by resentment, fierce in defensiveness
Ready to burn it all down
But, I'm not the exception, neither are you
No matter how righteous
Regardless how faithful
No magic prayer shields
No incantation protects
For, I'm not the exception, neither are you
World shakes, I stagger, you stagger too
Frailty stalks, I stumble, you stumble too
Grief intrudes, I sorrow, you sorrow too
There's no immunity, no immunity at all

Night haunts, night harrows
Insistent, night approaches
Always, always, night comes
No, I'm not the exception, neither are you.

But quiet, rising, awareness grows
Mysteriously led, I'm accompanied
Slowly, hope steadies
Received, trust deepens
I'm valued, I'm beloved
I'm drawn, I'm sought
I'm found, I'm held
I'm included, I'm welcomed
Bewildered by grace, enthusiastically forgiven
I'm not the exception, no, not the exception
I'm not the exception, neither are you.

Expelled

When they heard this, all in the synagogue were filled with wrath. And they rose up and put him out of the city.

Luke 4:28-29

Ever been put out
Ever driven out of camp
Singled out, scapegoated, ever been run off
Made an offense, labeled violation
Intolerable, for stating different opinion
For integrity, for living your truth
For just being Imago Dei, your sacred self
Ever been unwelcomed
Till pack your bags
Till shake the dust
Just shake the dust, leave, till walk away.

Sorry, but you're not alone
Sorry, but join outcast crowd
Great company of renegades
Membership irrationally accused
Sorry, but you're not alone
Sorry, but join Jesus
Kicked out of synagogue
That's right, Jesus
Chased from home town
Banned, deadly mob rising
Deadly mob on his heels.

Ever been put out
Ever driven from the camp
Sorry, but you're not alone
Sorry, but join Jesus on the run
Sometimes, complying's price too high

Conformity's cost excessive
Pretense moral compromise.

Ever been put out
Ever driven from camp
"Blessed are you," Jesus says
Yes, surprising, "Blessed are you"
For though devastating, though painful
Sometimes sorrowful, even harrowing
But blessed, for what if it's liberation
Yes, what if it's liberation
Points, at last, toward welcome
Drawn, at last, toward truest home.

Extravagant Sign

Husbands, love your wives, just as Christ also loved the
church and gave Himself up for her.

Ephesians 5:25

They say they will love, comfort, honor each other
to the end of their days. They say they will cherish
each other and be faithful to each other always.
They say they will do these things not just when
they feel like it, but even-for better for worse, for
richer for poorer, in sickness and in health-when
they don't feel like it at all. In other words, the vows
they make at a marriage could hardly be more
extravagant.

Frederick Buechner in WHISTLING IN THE
DARK

She's failing
Her illness, mysterious, more insidious
Her limitation more pronounced
She's failing
Trembling, so frail, holds on, grips tightly his arm
Slowly, so slowly shuffles into holy place
She's failing
Wonder bewildered, how does he manage, not just Sunday
How manage daily, carry constant, desperate dependency
She's failing
But seated close, so close, few minutes seated, settle side by side
Transformed, head on his shoulder, calmed, like miracle, she sleeps
She's failing
The way of all flesh, she's failing, but keeps his promises
Keeps old, impossible, keeps extravagant promises

She's failing
But quietly, so quietly, sign trustworthy, light faithful
He bears witness
Shines, he shines like the sun.
Eye to Eye with Jesus

Face to face with Christ my Savior
Face to face what shall it be

Interruption: It Might Be Just the Point

"For I was hungry and you gave me food…"
Matthew 25:35

It might be about as close as I ever get to Jesus, at least while confined to this rapidly crumbling, this frail mortality. The disheveled, unshaven face suddenly, unexpectedly appears at my office door. "Hey, are you the chaplain? Somebody told me you could get me something to eat…" I am not sure how they know, but you better believe that encounter happens at absolutely the most inconvenient time; just when there are about a dozen other things going on or I am about to pack up my things and head for the car at the end of the day. "Hey Chaplain…are you the Chaplain?" And Jesus shows up needy, hungry, demanding, expecting, as intrusive, as impossible as he can be. It might be I am never closer to Jesus than when filling out a free lunch ticket, explaining how the rules work, because it seems you really cannot trust Jesus to not take advantage, testing the limits, manipulating the system. It might be about as close as I ever get to Jesus, and yet, there is no time when I am more frustrated, more cynical, more suspicious, convinced I am not getting the whole story. Jesus will get you in trouble, disorient you, tangle you up in some complicated spot you would never have chosen on your own, some place you would rather not be.

Jesus might walk and talk with some of us in the lovely garden, but, lately anyway, Jesus has the bad habit of barging in, intruding in the messy middle of things; showing up gritty, intimidating, with "no place to lay his head," and his hand out, needing a meal, a shower, change of clothes, a whole list most of us could not imagine living without. Eye to eye with Jesus is a helpless, humbling place to be. The haunting reflection I see in his blood-shot gaze reminds me I have a long way to go.

Failed Again

Seeing Jerry's name show up on the old Baptist Hospital Facebook page brought a long-ago Sunday morning back to me. I was on call and had been asked to see a patient whose family member needed a meal pass. I always struggle with calls like this, never certain the need is real, mindful of limited resources, uncomfortably imagining how embarrassing it can be to be to have to ask for help. So, I arrived on the scene with my usual dis-ease and things pretty quickly got worse. The air was thick with cigarette smoke, and there were two young men needing a meal pass rather than one, neither of whom were family, but buddies who helped each other survive on the street, only too happy to hang out in the hospital till their friend was discharged. I navigated that as best I could, impatience and resentment rising, and then as I was leaving, attempted to lay down the law. "Look, we will do this one time and one time only, and while you are here you cannot be smoking in the room." "No one's been smoking here, " the quick sarcastic reply and that's when…well, that's when I raised my voice. Not quite sure what I said - as I recall something about being lied to – but whatever, it was angry and loud enough to be heard all the way down to the nurse's station.

Reflecting on that tense exchange from this perspective I know now, those guys in the room were much better at this sort of thing than I was – for them the first concern was something I failed to fully comprehend, it was survival – and I am quite sure at that moment I became just like every other clueless, patronizing, helper they had found a way to manipulate over the years. No matter how self-righteous I felt, on a deep level I knew I missed the point – their tragic need to deceive and how trapped they were in that, and my determination to add to their shame. I am guessing they felt some satisfaction watching me lose my cool. I can see now it was absurd.

As I left the floor in a huff, one of the nurses at the desk said, "Wow, Dan, did not know you could get that angry." At which time, Jerry, the gentle, peacemaking soul he is replied, "It's alright Dan, even Jesus got mad." "Yeah," I responded sourly, "But look what happened to him." And to my great relief, Jerry and the group sitting at the desk, laughed.

Fret Not!

This morning on my commute to work I did something either very brave or very foolish, something besides joining all the others denying their mortality, speeding up the Pellissippi Dragway in pre-dawn darkness. This morning I dared to turn on the news. I have not been doing that as much the last few years, preferring to read the news, giving a little control over the way the news assaults. But it was Friday and I really enjoy "Story Corps," a regular part of the end of the week broadcast on "Morning Edition." It was a mistake, listening to the news that is. I should have known better. I did not even make it to "Story Corps" till I was so much in a snit, I turned the broadcast off, disgusted. Steaming, muttering, "I cannot wait to get to my desk and tear off a raging rebuke. Those scoundrels have it coming!" So, once in the office I grabbed my journal and scalded the "dirtballs" with a whole page illegible scrawl.

However, work time was approaching and hoping to at least try to get my mind and spirit right, I picked up a devotional book I use only to encounter Psalm 37:7. Fret not! I hesitate to blame this on God, but do wonder if there might have been a little divine enjoyment of the chagrined shock, the jarring perspective the old poem delivered to my system. The ancient spiritual guide snatched my attention, seemingly speaking right to me, leaving me feeling self-consciously amused and more than a little exposed. "Don't waste your angst. It's futile. No one is interested in a lot of overheated, self-righteous rhetoric - we are drowning in it already. And besides, it makes no difference in the long run. The dirtballs always appear to prosper, always. Fret not! The evildoers know that game better than you do. Fret not! Somethings just are not worth your limited, precious time. Be still. Wait patiently. Take a breath, a deep breath. Watch. Remember who has the last word. Fret not!"

Though I am terrible at practicing this wisdom, though it remains beyond me, far beyond me, for I am an excellent "fretter," at least for a moment, a grace-filled, uncomfortable moment, the Psalmist saved me from myself. Made my morning.

Getting Around To It

And Jesus said to her, "O woman, what have you to do with me? My hour has not yet come."

John 2:4

"The life I touch for good or ill will touch another life, and in turn another, until who knows where the trembling stops or in what far place my touch will be felt."

Frederick Buechner in THE HUNGERING DARK

Jesus gets around to it
Changes his mind, Jesus starts something
Waiting, waiting, standing quietly on edge
Listening?
Discerning?
Maybe, counting the cost
Even Jesus needs a push
Hesitant?
Careful?
Grumpy, so grumpy in resistance
Yes, even Jesus needs a push
Who doesn't?
But finally, slowly
Long last, compelled
Long last, shoved into his moment
Jesus gets around to it
Changes his mind, Jesus starts something.

And so, it begins, it builds
Mysterious momentum of all eternity
His slow tending

His slow emptying
His slow dying
And so, it begins, it builds
His daunting
His reckless denial
Jesus sets his face, his haunted face
Bearing light against harrowing darkness
Scorned, laying down life for least of these
And so, it seems to end
In suffering death
In utter defeat, it all seems to end.

And yet, resurrection
And yet, unexpected
And yet, another beginning
Each new morning, begins again
And so, it continues
Listen, the world waits
Look, the heaving world waits
Stranded, cruelly bound
Still battered by harrowing darkness
Waits re-creation
Waits liberation
Waits revealing of children of God
World waits for us, still waits for us
Waits for you and me to get around to it.

And so it begins, it builds
Each new morning, begins again
And so it continues
Astounding, we are the light
We are the light of the world
Trembling, struggling
We are the flawed
In at least a thousand ways
Myriad, great and small, now, right now
Even on this day

We are the light of the world.

World waits
World waits for us, still waits for us
Waits for you and me to get around to it
Start something.

Good Trouble

"But she was greatly troubled at the saying."

Luke 1:29

"I got whomped upside the heart this morning."

Sister Margaret Turk

"Old monks are wild as well as simple. They perch more lightly on the globe than the rest of us."

Peter Levi in THE FRONTIERS OF PARADISE

News of Sister Margaret's death put me back in the early morning hallway at old Saint Mary's several years ago, confronted, sharing a sacred moment of wonderful bewilderment with my friend. I wish I could remember the particulars, whatever it was surprising and disturbing Sister Margaret, filling her with a kind of baffled awe. Something unexpected happened on her patient rounds. Sadly, the details are long gone from my faulty memory, but I pray I will never forget her humorous, honest confession. "I got whomped upside the heart this morning." And I hope I always recall her determination to make sense out of that encounter, to learn, to grow from it. In fact, there was something of excitement, of delight in her tone as she described a situation where she was uncertain what to do next. Whatever occurred had not been comfortable, but already she was leaning into the lesson she was certain it held, a look of anticipation, courageous, mystified joy on her face, wholly committed to wringing every bit of good she could out of it. I am sure I will be holding that image in my heart for a long time.

What troubles us? Whatever it is, I hope we find the nerve to pay attention, give deep consideration, to listen, to wrestle, battling to understand. Because, as the wise old pastor, John Ames, reminds in

Marilynne Robinson's wonderful novel GILEAD, "The worst misfortune isn't only misfortune." I know this is hazardous spiritual territory, perilously close to discounting the senseless horror too many face, but I trust, sometimes misfortune, sometimes trouble, as maddening as both can be, open the door for the remaking, laboring work of our redemptive God, always ready to break into our well defended worlds, whomping us upside our hearts. Like Mary, like our friend Sister Margaret, whose witness forever surrounds us, calling us ahead, be brave, pay openhearted, yet stubborn attention, for you might be surprised, blessed by, even startled by gift, by grace even in the chaos.

Just get in the way…get in good trouble.

John Lewis, Congressman from Georgia and Civil Rights Leader

Guide

I know how to be abased, and I know how to abound; in any and all circumstances I have learned the secret of facing plenty and hunger, abundance and want.

Philippians 4:12

Be still and know that I am God.

Psalm 46:10

"Only now she has become still enough to hear."

Wendell Berry in A PLACE ON EARTH

Struggles to speak
Vocabulary, few strained, few clipped words
Cannot walk
Doesn't feel whole right side, not in long, long time
But he hears
Yes, through stillness hears, seems hears rarest secret
Perhaps, by necessity learned to hear deeply
Suspect hears what I can't hear
Hears sound of joy resilient
Delight, quick smile, bright laugh tells me so
But he hears
Yes, through stillness hears, seems hears rarest secret
Perhaps, by necessity learned to hear deeply
Suspect hears what I can't hear
Hears sound of connections' blessing
Unearned welcome, extended left hand tells me so
He's remarkably steadfast, unreasonably consistent
Seemingly, radiantly, always the same.

Hope seen is not hope, Paul claims

But, beg to differ, I've seen it
Seen in wheelchair powered breathless down hallway
Seen openhearted, looking, looking, always looking
Alert to what's next, engaging newest day
So, apologies Paul, hope's seeable, I've seen it
Yes, right where never expected to see.

For, in quiet, hears
Yes, hears what I cannot hear
In helpless still, knows
Yes, knows what I have yet to know
Beyond easy understanding
No rational explanation
A wonder? A gift?
Yes, but more, can't leave it at that
How about witness, our instructor
Imagine out of quietest darkness
Imagine incomprehensible
Imagine grace's brilliant sign.

Came to keep you company, friend
That, as always, my intent
But over and over, aspiration upended
For, over and over, blessing's mine
Thank you, yes, blessing's all mine.

Heart Gets Bigger

Greater love has no man than this, that a man lay down his life for his friends.

John 15:13

"As your heart gets bigger on the inside, the world gets bigger on the outside."

Wendell Berry in "Stand By Me"

We suspect, Lord, it's no simple thing
No comfortable, no casual undertaking
This entangling, this messy love you call to emulate
Though tempted to quickly dismiss as foolhardy
To ignore, hoping all goes quietly away
Insistent, it troubles, there's uneasy recognition
Even strangely, a mysterious stirring
For glimpse daring, sense great company traveling
Navalny, Bonhoeffer, there's King, and Gandhi, too
Brothers in adversity, bold resisters of tyranny
Faces set, resolute, they listen
Then hearing, they follow better, more decent way
Defiant, like so many, determined faces inspiring
Countering violence, withering self-obsession
Generous signs standing, bravely bearing witness
Serving, intentional, accept staggering cost
Laying it down, they lay it all down
Lay down precious, precious lives
Devoted, pursuing your dream, Lord
Your great hope for healing broken world.

May their memory be a blessing, Lord
Stunning faithfulness our guide
Their open hearts steady, deepening insight
Their examples forever reminders
Releasing personal agenda
Sacrifice for love's sake
Laying down lives for love's sake
Slowly reveals deepest purpose
Uncovers truest, most abundant life.
Grant us courage.

Amen.

Response to 1 Corinthians 13:13

So faith, hope, love abide, these three; but the greatest of these is love.

When dust settles, finally settles
Shifting, trembling ground still at last
When lurching destruction quiets
What abides? What stands?

When change intrudes, disrupts
Chaos mocks, havoc bullies
When time's pace breathless
What abides? What remains?

What can we count on, God?
For leery, for hesitant to trust
Regret ridden, confidence wasted
Invested plans, dearest dreams
Opened hearts, but disappointed
Hopes shattered, casually betrayed
Abandoned by flimsy, fleeting loyalties
Transient causes, selfish leaders
Posturing, promising, but not delivering
They wither, decay, they die
Exposed empty, they do not abide
So, what continues? What persists?

O God who is love
Steadfast, relentless, eternity's witness
Present today, faithful all days to come
Deepen assurance, renew hope
Though whole creation shakes
We scramble, frantic for shelter
Though darkness threatens
We stumble perplexing path
Though strength falters
Our hearts stagger, spirits worn

Though lives frail, brief morning mist
Grief stalks, strikes, suddenly near
Though battered, your love endures
Though despised, your love perseveres
Though spurned, your love abides
Raised high against darkest night
Still standing, still overcoming
Nothing separates from you
Abiding, yes, your love abides.

Amen.

Response to 1 Corinthians 15:58

Be steadfast, immovable, always abounding in the work of the Lord,
knowing that in the Lord your labor is not in vain.

What abounds?
Uncontained, defies measure, any measure
What overflows?
What does my small life declare?
Question intimidates, Lord
Leary of revelation, rattled by exposure
Perhaps potential unmet, promises unkept
Haunting regret, wearying, emptying shame
Great effort, yet little, so little to show
Mindful, regardless devotion
Stability does not define me
Conscious, regardless determination
Steadiness escapes
Surrender creeps near
Mocking, lurking on horizon.

Reform understanding, Lord
Although you call to partnership
Embracing whole weary world
Searching for what is lost
Sustaining, renewing, relentless recreator
Who am I to presume?
Who am I to do your work?

Braced against despair
Uncertain of meaning
Remind, Lord, though task daunting
Stepping quickly over my head
Remind, it is your work
Your ceaseless labor
Tireless, you pursue fulfillment
Lifting on redemption's rising tide
Drawing toward end I cannot see

Deepen trust there's no tenderness
There's no kindness
No work of grace placed in your hands
No matter how minute, how flawed
How seemingly insignificant
No act of love wasted, ever lost to you
Forever remembered, forever blessed
In you, Lord, life abounds.

Amen.

Response to 1 John 3:1

See what love the Father has given us, that we should be
called the children of God.

We don't know, not deeply
We can't conceive, not fully
Struggle to accept, to receive
Hardly aware who we are
Clueless what we shall be
But gradually, haltingly, so slowly
Spirit uncovers, heart informs
Rouses, revealing true identity
Finally glimpsed, like passing hunch
Sensing hope, wondrous, even startling
For we are sought, we are marked
Made for love, your love, Lord, your love
Abiding, eternal, beyond imagining
Most profound, inexhaustible purpose
We are family, your wide family
Made for welcome, always welcome
Celebrated, desired, held in your embrace
All cherished, all included
Pressed close, joined by mercy
Why, we are children, your little children
Look! See what the Father has given us?
A wonder.

But for some, Lord, for many, too many
Some lost, ragged, some wandering souls
Humiliated, uncertain, wearied by shame
Some battered, used, some abused
Some blind, proud, willfully astray
Convinced unacceptable, far from worthy
For some Lord, for many, too many
For some, light breaks, but slowly, so slowly
Limping, staggered, bearing regret
Receiving, but ambivalent, but uneasy

Yet, still awakening bit by painful bit
Yet, belonging, no matter, yet, still belonging
For pursued, found, we are named
Regardless foolishness, called, still called
Called, not just any name
But holy, delight-filled, name of longing hope
Named love bestowed, named "Children of God"
Look! See what the Father has given us?
A wonder.

Amen.

Response to 1 John 4:4

Little children, you are of God and have overcome them;
for he who is in you is greater than he who is in the world.

World rises, seizes, world demands attention, Lord
Fascinating, yet disruptive
Scrambling perspective, we ignore, if possible
But, startling, intruding
Suddenly, nothing more crucial
More urgent, singular in requirement
Disturbing, haunting, then shaking from sleep
Dominating, filling every waking thought
Stalking, menacing chaos
Some imagined, but some real, too real
Some fabricated, but some substantive
Disaster's building, gnawing prospect
Till dread fills, balance falters
Till overwhelmed, convinced unequal to task.

For, we are as children, Lord
Little children
Some know, some know very well
But some do not, some refuse to know
Naïve, some self-absorbed
Yet, more anxious, more exposed
More needy than care to admit
We are as children, little children
Pretending, posturing
Strategic in denial, distracting by design.

Remind, Lord, though children
Though little children
We're not helpless, we're not alone
Though world threatens to overpower
Roaring destructive, terrifying in might
Though children, yet, we are your children
And whatever disturbs, whatever horrifies

Whatever discourages, whatever confuses
Whatever assaults, whatever obstructs
Whatever poised, ready to drive down
Whatever it is, you are greater
Whatever it is, you overcome
Yours the final word
Nothing separates from your love
Nothing in all creation, not one thing.

Amen.

Response to 2 Corinthians 3:17

*Now the Lord is the Spirit, and where the Spirit of the Lord is,
there is freedom.*

Close as breath, then next breath
Near as heart beat, then next heart beat
Lord of longing's eternal labor
Never resting, tending, birthing
You, our waker, deliverer, our enabler
All creation, teems, charged
Vibrant with liberation's hope
And wherever you are
Where Spirit broods, then resides
Where Spirit blows, then intrudes
Where Spirit is, right there, in very place
Where Spirit is, freedom overflows.

Lift wonder, Lord, stir expectation
For we are weary, often beaten down
Diminished by brutal chaos
Betrayed by fear-filled hearts
Be patient, Lord
Sharpen awareness, remind
Where Spirit abides
Oppression doomed, one day ends
Where Spirit abides
Tribalism doomed, one day ends
Where Spirit abides
Violence doomed, one day ends
Where Spirit abides
Greed doomed, one day ends
Where Spirit abides
Love's voice fills, lifts unhindered
Reconciliation's project plows ahead
Where Spirit abides
Joy stands tall, then stands again
Glad song resilient, outlasting night

Where Spirit abides
Peace bids, draws, peace gathers
All your children, received, all welcomed
All joined one to another.

Bring that day, Lord, bring it quickly
We watch, hungering, we thirst
Leaning to very edge
Make us free, Lord, make us free.

Amen.

Response to 2 Corinthians 4:7

But we have this treasure in earthen vessels

Lord, we hardly realize
Hardly comprehend what we have
So rare, so transcendent, why, a treasure
This treasure indescribable
Your love, persistent, your labor, re-creative
Unhindered, uncontained, loose in the world
Moving, prompting, touching deepest place
Though ignored, though misunderstood
Driven to edge, used for selfish gain
Yet, persevering, yet bearing witness
Through every terror dared imagined
Sinister, delighting in destruction
Resilient, light piercing darkest night
Inextinguishable, shining on
Darkness comprehends it not
That's what we have.

Stir awe, Lord, awaken gratitude
For, tend to make it all about us
Masters of our little universe
Acquiring, accumulating, so entitled
Driven by self-promotion's hubris
Defending small, narrow lives
Yet, all the while, fragile, flawed
So weak, wounded, so sick and sore
Hiding truth, our whole truth
Frail, transient as can be.

But, wonder, yes wonder still abides
For we have this, though astounded
We have this treasure not by merit
Not earned, not achieved
But, we have this treasure
Bestowed, received

Ours by grace, by stunning favor.

Grant humility, Lord
Stretching wide needy hands
Opening rigid, fearful hearts
Weary vessels raised, remade
Your struggling, earthy children
Beloved, held, shining like the sun.

Amen.

Response to Amos 5:24

*But let justice roll down like waters, and righteousness like
an ever-flowing stream.*

Lord, your justice overflows
Slowly, inexorably, bit by bit
Exposing barriers to fairness
Breaching privilege's presumption
Crumbling dehumanizing structures
Challenge vision, raise hope
One day, justice shall overcome.

Lord of right relation's healing flood
Unrelenting, unrestricted
Confronting oppression

Conceiving liberation
Embracing disenfranchised
Challenge vision, raise hope
One day righteousness shall overcome.

But what about today, Lord?
What about "fierce urgency of now?"
Dare I pray, "let justice roll down?"
Dare I cry, "let righteousness flow?"
I hesitate, nerve falters
For if stand with you, Lord
Proclaiming justice, promoting righteousness
If stand with you, risk intimidates
Scrambling status quo
Exposing my self-centered world
My blindness to suffering
My intolerance, my fear
My greed and defensiveness
Entitled, regardless damage
Stand with you, it's costly
Stand with you, and forever changed.

But who affords apathy?
Justify, rationalize doing nothing?
Excuse looking away
Consequence rises up
Reminding, disturbing, rising again
Devastating spirit, eroding soul
So, though unequal to the task
Hardly grasping hazardous path
Grant courage, Lord
Courage to stand with you
Captured by your difficult dream
Your partner practicing resurrection
Trusting, regardless wasting violence
Regardless entrenched bigotry
Nevertheless, justice shall come
Your righteousness on the way
Rolling down, swept along
Borne ahead on love's redeeming tide.

Amen.

Response to Deuteronomy 30:14

But the word is very near you; it is in your mouth and in your heart, so that you can do it.

If you're close, Lord, so very close
Imminent, surrounding, pressing in
Near as next breath, next thought
If you're close, why so elusive?
Absent, just absent
Silent, so silent when needed most
If you're close, why this loneliness?
This stumbling, this empty chaos
If you're so close, Lord
Already in my mouth, my heart
Inhabiting my words, my dreams
If you're close, why this hunger?
This longing, this incessant thirst
If you're close, why this restlessness?
This discontent, this frantic searching
If you're so close.

Quiet me, Lord, reassure
Though doubts unnerve
Fears threaten, terrors shake
Uncertainty clouds my way
Grant compassion, kinder awareness
This blundering, this stumbling journey
Wayward floundering toward meaning
While maddening, while disconcerting
Blessed, sacred sign, holy struggle
For nothing separates from you
Not questions, despair, not crushing defeat
Instead, each alive, teeming with possibility
Mystery-filled, beckoning , drawing toward home
For hand extended in darkness, your hand
Voice above storm, your voice
For all belongs to you

All contained in your love
Redemptive, reckless, your sacrificial
Your total devotion
Approaching, pursuing to brink
Defying any limit, seeking, finding, lifting
Carrying with foolishness of grace
Patiently bearing till trust takes root
Everything, every little thing I need
Every thing I need is here.

Amen.

Response to Ezekiel 36:26

I will give you a new heart and put a new spirit in you;
I will remove from you your heart of stone and give you a heart of flesh.

God our creator
Constantly renewing, ceaselessly restoring
Resolute, determined, making whole
God of recreating, redemptive love
Hear our prayer.

We confess
We're people with damaged hearts
Hardened, wearied, often afraid
Crippling cynicism, intolerance, hollowing greed
Broken by betrayal, grief, so much more
We're people with damaged hearts
Staggering, bewildered in darkness
Crushed, heavy with disappointment
Struggling to believe anything ever changes.

Transforming God, refocus vision
Till glimpse, till see in what seems only decay
Though pinned by oppressing despair
Trust resilient, trust surprises
Trust you haven't given up
Love urges ahead, moving undeterred
Eroding, wearing away
Shattering hearts of stone
Bit by bit making new
Transforming God, stir expectation
Till hear persistent, hear persevering
Voice penetrating, overcoming darkness
Still, small, ceaselessly calling by name
Reforming shadowy chaos, creating a world
Bit by bit making new.

God of grace, patient, eternally patient
Brighter day's stubborn commit
Steady hearts, give daring
Joyfully embracing your determination
Receiving, marked by your remaking
Longing, bravely expecting
Wherever you labor, hope's born
Gently held, broken hearts healed
Bit by bit making new.

Amen.

Response to Galatians 3:28

There is neither Jew nor Greek, there is neither slave nor free, there is neither male nor female; for you are all one in Christ Jesus.

God, OUR Father
We speak more truth than we know
More, far more than acknowledged,
More than till this very day practiced
Unconsciously calling you, "OUR Father"
Mindless habit, routine holy mumble
Hardly aware, if you're OUR father
Not just my father, but OUR father
If you're OUR father, then next person
Next face, any face, regardless of difference
Each encounter, yours as well
All the living, every one of us.

God, OUR Father
We've done it again, over then over again
Reckless heresy's agents of destruction
Fears of difference, haunt, they blind
Exalting bigotry, boosting disrespect
Promoting evil's loudest voice
Bullying, degrading till glorying worst selves
Wrecking your great hope, breaking your heart
Cost staggering, price incalculable
Forgive foolish ways.

God OUR Father
Surrounded by witness to better way
Lifted by bold dreamers
Risky faithful, brightening sacrifice
Devastating many, some known only to you
Move us, inspire us, deepen determination
For sacred work, your work, far from finished
Fill labor with daring openheartedness
Bravely following till your kingdom comes

At last living into own words, your great hope
At last liberated from fear-filled intolerance
Vision redeemed, healed by wide welcome
At last seeing more than difference
More even than brother, than sister
Seeing clearly, seeing simply your child
Created miracle, filled with your image
Infinitely loved, worthy respect
Precious in your sight.
Amen.

Response to Galatians 6:9

And let us not grow weary in well-doing, for in due season we shall reap, if we do not lose heart.

Regardless stubborn resistance, Lord
How loudly raise protest
How desperately pretend otherwise
Weariness descends unbidden
Even fortifying best intentions
Rigorous determination
Passion to make a difference
Energy falters, fades…dreams dim, die.

Tired, Lord, weak, Lord, I am worn
Where once hopeful
Now, spent, near completely spent
Violence depletes, despair damages
Disrespect devastates, demands due
Where once expectant
Now, despairing, now, almost broken
Sucked under by suspicion, by intolerance
Howling fear, wasting defensiveness
Driven down, then driven down again
Battered by whole weary world.

Yet, your call perseveres, Lord, insistent
Challenging, "Do not grow weary"
Deepening resolve to do good
Resist losing heart
Patiently labor toward your better day
But how? Staggered far beyond any limit.

Remind, though few walk well-doing's path
Though narrow, near abandoned
Startled, I find you there, Lord
You, among hungry, imprisoned, sick, bereft
You, accompanying, joyful in partnership
Embracing all creation with redemptive love

Though struggle seems endless
Remind, this too shall pass
For the work, the future is yours
Though wounded, crushed in spirit
Though strength flees, my way lost
Relentless, you do not quit
You seek, draw near, you lift up
Tenderly carry toward home.

Amen.

Response to Isaiah 9:2

The people who walked in darkness have seen a great light; those who dwelt in a land of deep darkness, on them has a light shined.

God of light, great light
Laboring, light disturbing
Pushing back harrowing night
No darkness in you, no darkness at all
Persevere, fill our dark land
Make bright dark lives.

We know, God, resist admitting, but know
We are too comfortable, too much at home in night
Accommodating shadowy intolerance and fear
Haunted by violence, by vengeance
Diminishing selfishness, waste, much more
This, our lonely, soul-withering night
Eroding hope, blocking dreams
Frustrating gracious liberation
This, our deep darkness
These our shadows
We know them
Know them well, too well.

Hungry for light, we long, we search
But ambivalent, near anxious
Suspecting, on some level fearing
Afraid light will over-power, will expose
Illumine shame-filled corners long ignored
Secrets prefer hidden, remain hidden
Requiring more honest, more humble ways.

God of light, grant courage
Till bravely shaking off pretense

Boldly trusting received just as we are
Aware, though seeing flaws, you reach
Welcome wide, sought without limit
Recklessly approaching, heedlessly risking
Entering, redeeming, you remake our chaos
Bearing brokenness, lifting heavy need
Never abandoning, never forsaking
You accompany through
All the way through darkest night.

God of great light, incomprehensible light
Breath catches, we wait, we watch
Hope birthing, hope rising
Glimpsing dawn-break's declaration.

Amen.

Response to Isaiah 11:6

The wolf shall dwell with the lamb, and the leopard shall lie down with the kid, and the calf and the lion and the fatling together, and a little child shall lead them.

Your words bewilder, Lord, exceed imagining
In world's warring, world's senseless slaughter
Lives toxic, narrowed, deadly with mistrust
Glorying intolerance, devouring, belittling
How do I find your way, understand prompting?
Little about your vision, almost nothing, familiar
Except, perhaps this, yes, this one thing
This quiet nudging, this insistent
Heart's troubling, yet, longing, still longing witness
Ancient question, "Can it possibly be true?"

But dare risk hope's burden again?
Muster audacity, re-awaken foolishness?
For hoped before, Lord, yes, hoped it all before
Dreaming, working, trust rebuilt
Excitement rising, but staggered, then crashing
Brought down again, cynicism triumphs again
Cussedness tramples, vengeance triumphs, fear intimidates
So, dare embrace your dream one more time?
Probably not, Lord, not today, not now midst rubble
Not now midst terror, midst ruthless slaughter, midst death
For now, believing breaks hearts, now, compassion crushes.

Yet, there's no denying restless searching
No silencing still, small, no silencing your determined voice
Appealing to stubborn, to tenacious hope
Your resilient, your enduring vision
Eternal longing for unity, for peace on Earth
Remind, Lord, you dwell deep
Grappling, you enter, you work harrowing trenches
Remind wherever kindness, wherever healing moves
You are there, you are already there

Wherever understanding stirs, wherever empathy rises
You are there, you are already there
Wherever redemption, wherever re-creation struggles ahead
You are there, you are already there
Wherever justice stands, wherever mercy served
You are there, you are already there
Wherever cause worthy of our lives
You are already there, laboring righteousness
Disturbing, drawing, your dream on the way.

Can it be true, Lord
Can it possibly be true?
Make it so
Only you can make it so.

Amen.

Response to Isaiah 25:4

For thou hast been a stronghold to the poor, a stronghold to the needy in his distress, a shelter from the storm and a shade from the heat; for the blast of the ruthless is like a storm against a wall.

Finally sinks in, Lord, registers at last
Slow, uneasy, disconcerting awareness
Eroding, exposing, overwhelming defenses
Till acknowledge, till slowly, grudgingly admit
We fool ourselves, stalked by inevitable
Ruthlessness pursuing, gaining
Yet, proud, yet, defensive
Dig in, we double-down, desperate in pretense
Blustering, bullying, anxious, we hide vulnerability
Hoping against hope, all goes away, just goes away
But, try as we might, denying, posturing
Storms howling, battering plans
Trials blistering, scorching dreams
Till at last, trapped, broken, at last exhausted
Finally, we know, finally know it is true
Know we are no match.

Great deliverer
You are stronghold, Lord
Rising, like mighty wall surrounding
Resisting ruthless, battling foes
You, Lord, our stronghold
Remind, lest we forget
Grace inhabits our stories
Deliver again, Lord, set free
And you are shelter, Lord
Shielding, protecting
Defending when unable to stand
You, Lord, our shelter
Remind, lest lose our way
Grace accompanies our stories

Deliver again, Lord, set free
And you are shade, Lord
Refreshing, renewing
Cover through parched, barren land
You, Lord, our shade
Remind, lest despair defeats
Grace redeems our stories
Deliver again, Lord, set free
Though poor, needy, still watching, still hoping
We wait for you, Lord, we wait for you.

Amen.

Response to Isaiah 40:3

A voice cries: "In the wilderness prepare the way of the Lord,
make straight in the desert a highway for our God."

Lord you call
Patient, call persistent
Raising your voice wherever I am
Even here, call in maddening wilderness
You speak deep into chaotic darkness
Awaken longing, you call my name
Then call again, then call again.

But I struggle to listen, Lord
Distracted, desperate for satisfaction
Convinced wealth is answer
Grasping more, building portfolio
Yet, emptiness rises, voice cries out
Then lured by safety's promise
Suspecting everyone, defending everywhere
Yet, uneasiness rises, insecurity haunts
Then persuaded pleasure fulfills
Seeking excitement, craving entertainment
Yet, discontent abides, troubling, demanding
For beneath frantic noise
Still, small voice, your voice, urging, drawing
Have mercy, I did not know it was you.

Lord you call, then keep calling
On the move
Steadfast, you move my direction
No matter how lost
How far off beaten path
Coming, coming, down into wilderness
You keep coming my way
Dismissive barriers
Regardless, prepared or not
Coming, coming, down into wilderness
You keep coming my way
Challenging rigid certainties

Preoccupying, narrow agendas
Relentless, you pursue
Seek till you find
Determined to capture my heart
Liberate my soul.

Lord you call. then keep calling
Patient, call persistent
I wait, ear pressed to ground
Wait restless, wait hungry,
Hungrier than I know.

Amen.

Response to Isaiah 49:16

Behold, I have graven you on the palms of my hands;
your walls are continually before me.

Lights dim, fade, floor gives way
Overwhelmed, we wrestle despair
Storm batters, ripping, tearing
Threatening to remain
Wounded, bewildered, we stagger
Near hopeless, convinced stranded
Forever tangled in wilderness
Where are you, Lord, where are you?
Startled, perplexed, we wonder
Almost cannot help but wonder.

Remind, Lord, inspire imagination
Till, little by little, we learn, we trust
Lengths of your steady compassion
Depths of indescribable love
Recklessly choosing, foolishly risking
You refuse safety from us
Marked, borne deep in very being
Driven, folded into, held in your great heart
Preposterous, who could suggest
Who suspects you might forget
Ever lose sight of love for us
Yet, we do, Lord, we often do
Almost cannot help but wonder.

So, next time, Lord, next time call to mind
Next time gloom descends
Next time terrified forsaken
Next time protest rises
Next time life lurches, nearly shatters
For next time sure to come
Lurking, mocking, stalking our way
So, call to mind

Names, our names, eternally etched
Cut, deeply cut, indelible
Graven in palms of your hands
Faithfully, call to mind
Your labor continues, perilous, passionate
Doing all the good you can possibly do
And keep calling to mind
For while you never forget, we do
Yes, we do, Lord, we often do.

Amen.

Response to Isaiah 53:4

Surely he has borne our griefs and carried our sorrows.

Bearer of griefs, carrier of sorrows
All our sorrows
Burdens oppress, eroding, they crush
Harassing, clinging, they accumulate
We stagger, Lord, strain, lift
Carry till carry no longer
Till crumble under impossible weight
But devastating, this heaviest of all
Most painful, most maddening
Grief's persistent emptiness
Sorrow's insistent ache
Dreams scattered, hopes crushed.

We battle, Lord, give best effort
Praying, ignoring, we even pretend
Shielding, we bind own wounds
Dragging shattered lives ahead
Yes, we try over, then over again
But now, weary, now, at last, spent
For, now we know
There are failures, there is trauma
Brokenness we cannot bear
Now we know, yes, but we struggle
Still scuffling to accept, to let go
Admit beyond capacity to control
For, now we know
Shame rises, dread batters, we fear
No one else wants this, Lord, not really
No one wants worn, hollow self
No one
No one but you, yes, no one but you.

Have patience, convince, that's enough
Your grace, Lord, your wide welcome

Enough, that's more than enough
For you approach where others turn away
Accompanying, you abide, then you stay
Committed, carrying sorrow at any cost
Determined, bearing grief regardless price
Receiving, you labor to redeem
Marked by comfort, held by overflowing love.

Amen.

Response to Isaiah 54:10

For the mountain may depart and the hills be removed, but my steadfast love shall not depart from you, and my covenant of peace shall not be removed says the Lord who has compassion on you.

Landmarks fade, Lord, disappear
Authority's source, truth's beacon
Everything familiar staggers
Lives tremble, stunned till disbelieving
Seeping, eroding, near collapse
Lives shake, spirits waver
Foundations heave, then crumble
What can we count on?
Where in the world is steady ground?
What stands when everything falls away?

Lord of love
Steadfast, trustworthy
Lord who has compassion on us
Moved by our struggle, affected by our fear
Could it be you?
You, our anchor, our rock?
Even if unimaginable intrudes
Even if mountains
Stately, awe inspiring
Even if mountains suddenly vanish
It is you who remains, resolute, committed
Compassionate always, no matter what
And even if hills
Powerful, proudly permanent
Even if hills bit by bit carried away
It is you who remains, solid, fixed
Faithful always, no matter what.

Remind, as chaos taunts
Ripping, tearing
Devouring much we need

Threatening all held in our hearts
Remind, though destruction roars
Mighty, intimidating
Though in own strength we are lost
For we are no match, no match at all
Though we stumble in shadows
Unfailing love seeks, draws nearer still
Compassion longs, holds fast
It is you, Lord, you never let go.

Amen.

Response to Isaiah 65:1

I was ready to be sought by those who did not ask for me;
I was ready to be found by those who did not seek me.

Long before knew what to ask
Puzzled, so perplexed
Unable to grasp
Unable to voice deepest need
You were ready
Hoping to hear us call, still hoping
Long before knew where to look
Unaware what we sought
Bewildered, so baffled
Strangers to ourselves
You were ready
Eager to be found, still eager
Our souls mute, spirits dazed
Yet stirred, yet awakened
Enlivened by revelation's labor
Faithful from the beginning
Faithful to the end.

Be patient, Lord
Understanding our complex lives
Mystifies, escapes
Discerning your mysterious ways
Daunting, so disorienting
Discouragement descends
Our path dark, our way lonely
Remind, Lord
You are ready, eager to take first step
Recklessly disregarding cost
You are ready, eager to seek when lost
Persevering till found
You are ready, eager to steady stumbling feet
Lifting when we fall, patiently lifting again
You are ready, eager to bear crushing burdens
Redeeming, you heal battered hearts

You are ready, eager to lead toward home
Drawing, holding all the way
You do not let go.

Long before we know
Before we know what to ask
Before we know where to seek
Long, yes long before we know
You are ready
Longing love loose in the world
Calling, urging
Never to leave us alone.

Amen.

Response to Jeremiah 29:7

But seek the welfare of the city where I have sent you into exile, and pray to the
Lord on its behalf,
for in its welfare you will find your welfare.

Lord, we flounder, trapped
Perplexed aliens exiled
Estranged from familiar
Anything seeming to make sense
Heaving world batters, takes breath
Resisting, we raise grievance, seed mistrust
Scramble defenses, regardless damage
Till crushed, spirits atrophy
Apostles hopeless alienation.

But tirelessly, but persistently
You call, Lord, then call again
Turning, nudging different direction
Quieting, you reassure, even in exile
Wonder wakes, reminding there's no place
No matter how intractable brokenness
How structured intolerance
There's no place, no matter how baffling
How complicated hopelessness
How entrenched self-destructiveness
There's no place you do not labor
Patient, resolutely redemptive
No place beyond love's re-creation
No place your light not shining
Raised high against darkest night.

But we struggle shaking uneasiness, Lord
Wary, you draw toward risky work
Do it, and we'll not be the same
Do it, and compassion deepens

Do it, and hearts grow larger
Fractured world slips into self-centered lives
Then slowly, near overwhelmed, we know
Almost against our will we know
Wherever woundedness
Wherever misery rages
Wherever misunderstanding intractable
Wherever despair locks it all up
Wherever disrespect tears it all down
Daring love leads there
Your great heart enters, abides right there.

Grant wisdom, Lord, give courage.

Amen

Response to Job 29:3

when his lamp shone upon my head, and by his light I walked through darkness;

Night returns, Lord, again, then again
Inevitable, unremitting, oppressing
Drawing near, enclosing, capturing
Night returns
So, settle, comforted in darkness
Though, my instinct to fight, to resist
Flee, be gone, far as far can be
Then mustering determination
Struggle, stretch, reach toward light
Labor to liberate, break myself free.

But, I've learned, Lord
Slowly, sometimes, painfully
Realizing, at last, my power insufficient
For darkness, menacing, chaotic
Coming, going, intruding at will
All my strength is no match at all.

So, once again, Lord, as gloom gathers
Taunting, intimidating, disorienting
Stirring anxious dread
Once again, settle, comforted in darkness
Quietly, calmly, till stillness informs
Till instructed, moved by experience
Recalling cycling despair's old lessons
Slipping, staggering, but still walking
Threatened, but not quite finished off
Accompanied on stumbling journey
Lamp, held high, illuminating, revealing
Overcoming darkness
Drawing steadfastly toward dawn.

Remind, raise hope, Lord

Grant, over and over, grant like before
Even in deepest night
Your brilliance inextinguishable
Still surrounding
Still steadying
Still holding
Still leading
Till back into light
Till in darkness no more.

Amen.

Response to John 1:5

The light shines in the darkness, and the darkness has not overcome it.

God, steady light
Our morning star
Illumine dim, stumbling paths
Push back threatening gloom
Shadows of selfishness, seething suspicion
Our fears, hopelessness, our despair
Push back small, dark impulses
Dimming, warring against your light
Defying your dream for all your children
Keep shining in our darkness.

As new day rises, God
Lift courage, daring trust
Determined listening through divisive racket
Till hearing, till finally moved by your good news
Where seeing only darkness, and we often do
Even there, in forsaken places
Even there you do not give up
Your persistent light still shines
Calling, leading toward your brighter day
When fearing darkness, and we often do
Ashamed of hidden failures
Intimidated by chaos
Cowered by power of illness, by frailty
Quiet trembling hands
Stir resilient, laboring hope
Trusting, big, bad as darkness might be
Beaten down as often feel
Darkness never overcomes
Never outlasts your commitment to light
For when darkness does its worst
When howling, destructive fury ceases
Your persistent light still shines
Calling, leading toward brighter day.

God, steady light
Keep shining in our darkness
We wait, we watch
Holding on through long, silent night
Morning star, light our world

Amen

www.ingramcontent.com/pod-product-compliance
Lightning Source LLC
Chambersburg PA
CBHW071001120626
46546CB00003B/885